The Nazi and Japanese Human Experimentation Programmes

I would like to acknowledge and offer my gratitude to Stacey Scuffell BSc (Hons/Biology) who has assisted in the production of this volume.

The Nazi and Japanese Human Experimentation Programmes

Biological War Crimes during WW2

Tim Heath

First published in Great Britain in 2024 by
Pen & Sword History
An imprint of Pen & Sword Books Limited
Yorkshire – Philadelphia

Copyright © Tim Heath 2024

ISBN 978 1 39908 209 9

The right of Tim Heath to be identified as
Author of this Work has been asserted by him in accordance
with the Copyright, Designs and Patents Act 1988.

A CIP catalogue record for this book is
available from the British Library

All rights reserved. No part of this book may be reproduced or
transmitted in any form or by any means, electronic or mechanical
including photocopying, recording or by any information storage and
retrieval system, without permission from the Publisher in writing.

Typeset by Mac Style
Printed in the UK by CPI Group (UK) Ltd, Croydon, CR0 4YY.

Pen & Sword Books Limited incorporates the imprints of After
the Battle, Atlas, Archaeology, Aviation, Discovery, Family History,
Fiction, History, Maritime, Military, Military Classics, Politics,
Select, Transport, True Crime, Air World, Frontline Publishing, Leo
Cooper, Remember When, Seaforth Publishing, The Praetorian Press,
Wharncliffe Local History, Wharncliffe Transport, Wharncliffe True
Crime and White Owl.

For a complete list of Pen & Sword titles please contact

PEN & SWORD BOOKS LIMITED
47 Church Street, Barnsley, South Yorkshire, S70 2AS, England
E-mail: enquiries@pen-and-sword.co.uk
Website: www.pen-and-sword.co.uk
or
PEN AND SWORD BOOKS
1950 Lawrence Road, Havertown, PA 19083, USA
E-mail: uspen-and-sword@casematepublishers.com
Website: www.penandswordbooks.com

Contents

Introduction		vii
Chapter 1	Cash for Corpses	1
Chapter 2	A Divine Apocalypse	4
Chapter 3	Human Guinea Pigs	19
Chapter 4	The Nazi Medical Experiments	22
Chapter 5	Aktion T4 – the Nazi Euthanasia Programme	61
Chapter 6	Elsa's Return	66
Chapter 7	The Nuremberg Doctors' Trial	70
Chapter 8	Human Taxidermy	92
Chapter 9	Imperial Japanese Human Medical Experimentation	110
Afterword		164
Acknowledgements		167
Bibliography		168

Introduction

Among the most appalling cruelties perpetrated throughout the course of the Second World War was undoubtedly that of medical and military experimentation conducted upon both living and deceased human beings. The various Nazi human experimentation programmes were initially carried out not so much in the pursuit of any particular scientific or medical discipline, but largely as a result of the Third Reich's obsession with race and eugenics. However, this criminal sub-discipline of the Nazi fascination with its warped racial ideologies was excused as little other than collateral damage by many of the Nazi physicians and their assistants involved in these practices.

Germany's Axis ally, the Japanese Empire, notorious for its cruelty and sadism even prior to the outbreak of the Second World War, ran its own independent programmes of human experimentation, the most infamous of these being known as 'Unit 731', where human beings were not only subject to the most appalling abuses, but were injected with cocktails of poisons and/or infected with diseases. In some instances they were dissected while fully conscious without any anaesthesia being administered beforehand. It can be said that both Third Reich Germany and Imperial Japan had a more or less inexhaustible supply of human guinea pigs throughout the Second World War to service the ghastly enterprise of human medical experimentation. These unfortunate souls consisted largely of concentration camp inmates or, in the case of the Japanese, the indigenous peoples of the lands they conquered, along with British, American, Indian and Australian prisoners of war.

Questions remain about the use of human experimentation by both regimes. What was the true purpose of these so-called experiments? What was the aim? And is there any evidence to suggest cooperation between Nazi Germany and the Japanese Empire in terms of the collation of data gained through the execution of these ghastly endeavours? This book examines these questions, as well as exploring why Japanese physicians involved in human experimentation and medical torture were excused indictment for war crimes, when the evidence against them was overwhelming. Furthermore, is there any truth in the suggestion that the Allied powers benefited from material obtained through interrogation carried out at the end of the Second World War? The complicity of both German and Japanese pharmaceutical companies must also be brought into question, as many cooperated willingly with the military, making handsome profits and continuing to do so long after the Second World War had ended.

This work is an attempt to answer these questions, drawing on the testimonies of perpetrators and victims found in many new first-hand and archival sources. It also serves as a horrifying and sobering reminder of man's capacity for inhumanity to fellow human beings, in the context of two brutal military regimes of the twentieth century.

'For the most part they are a nameless dead. To their murderers these wretched people were not individuals at all. They came in wholesale lot and were treated worse than animals awaiting slaughter'.
Brigadier General Telford Taylor, Chief of Counsel,
Nuremberg Doctors' Trial, 1945.

Chapter 1

Cash for Corpses

The utilisation of human beings as a resource for human medical experimentation is by no means a recent phenomenon. Although quite different in many aspects to that conducted throughout the Second World War by the Axis forces, it is worth some brief examination of the history of the subject of human medical experimentation in order to gain some historical perspective. From the earliest understanding of medical matters and primitive surgical practices for which there is a wealth of evidence, there were those who for whatever reason found themselves being procured as guinea pigs for what can only be described as quack treatments of one form or another, and, even worse, crude surgical procedures. As with the evidence of trepanation found in skulls of those long dead from the ancient world, there were some willing participants in early medicine seemingly happy to take part in extreme procedures, either in the hope that, as in modern times, their voluntary endeavours might provide something of value and contribute to saving lives in the future, or in desperate hope of relief from a condition for which there was then no treatment. Also there were individuals who were considered to be of less sound mind, who had little choice about their own fate.

In 1752 the British parliament passed the Murder Act, which permitted the bodies of executed criminals to be taken to the Company of Surgeons in London, where they were dissected for the purposes of medical and surgical study and teaching. In fact, seminars were held at which freshly hanged criminals cut down from the gibbet underwent dissection before a live audience of medical students. By the latter stages of the eighteenth century a cottage industry in body

2 The Nazi and Japanese Human Experimentation Programmes

snatching was spawned as a result of the demand for human corpses for medical dissection, due to the shortage of those that were legally available. Criminal gangs of 'resurrectionists' were particularly active in large cities such as London. The resurrectionists became highly adept at the exhumation of bodies from cemeteries and crypts. There were also cases in which doctors and pupils became embroiled in the theft of the dead in what was seen as an 'unholy' practice.

Famous characters such as Burke and Hare were entrepreneurs of a sort, supplying dead bodies to institutions such as Edinburgh's College of Medicine. The activities of this pair could have quite easily provided the inspiration for Mary Shelley's *Frankenstein*, but Burke and Hare were only too real. The infamous duo were not 'body snatchers', in the true sense of the term, but resorted to a form of 'murder to order' to fulfil the demand for corpses for medical purposes. While there were quite considerable amounts of money to be made, the criminals had few scruples, and they worked in the knowledge that there would be no questions asked of them upon the production of a body. Until the introduction of the Anatomy Act 1832 in Britain, the theft of corpses was not exactly illegal, as a corpse had no legal standing and was not owned by anyone. However, once a body had been stolen, it was illegal to dissect the corpse or to remove anything on the body, such as gold wedding rings or necklaces. Perhaps surprisingly, an initial attempt at introducing legislation to curb the practice of body snatching failed, despite being proposed by a committee of the House of Commons. It was clear to many on the committee that they were facing a widespread problem. The Royal College (formerly Company) of Surgeons in London was not happy about the proposal for change, or losing any of its privileges. It was even suggested that the bodies of the poor and destitute, rather than just convicted criminals, should be made available for dissection and/or anatomical study, which was strongly opposed by the Church as morally and religiously reprehensible. Nonetheless, the Anatomy Act of 1832 gave surgeons legal access to the remains of the deceased from workhouses, hospital morgues and prisons, provided that bodies were not claimed by the next-of-kin within forty-eight hours. It was also possible for a person to donate their next-of-kin's body for medical study. In modern society individuals can still donate their own bodies to science after death, and give permission for their organs to be used for transplant.

The scourge of grave robbery continued into the nineteenth century, despite legislation being introduced to curb the practice, along with severe sentences for those caught or otherwise associated with criminal acts. Gradually grave robbery and the procurement of the deceased for medical/surgical purposes became a thing of the past. However, with the outbreak of the Second World War in 1939, and the Nazi obsession with Aryanism, race and eugenics, medical experimentation on human beings took a far more terrifying and sinister twist.

The Nazis, as well as their later military ally the Japanese Empire, brought a new level of horror and cruelty to human medical experimentation. The medical experiments carried out by the Nazi German and Imperial Japanese regimes were not confined primarily to the butchery of cadavers, of those who had perished either in battle or while imprisoned, but were expanded to include live human beings. The catalogue of horrors which took place in the name of Nazi and Japanese racial theories has no equal in human history. While the Nazis were pursuing the virtues of their racial and Aryan science, the Japanese appeared to have little overall direction for the agonising and often fatal medical/surgical experiments carried out on unfortunate live victims. It seems that both regimes pursued medical experimentation with a high degree of vigour, sadism and pleasure, without any consideration for the physical and psychological wellbeing of the unfortunate victims.

Chapter 2

A Divine Apocalypse

As the Nazis assumed that they would win against the Allies to conclude the Second World War, Himmler had already discussed a proposal for the creation of a form of Nazi race and biology history museum in which organ specimens, bones, foetuses, skulls and more terrifying human taxidermy displays would grace vast marble halls in a celebration of the Aryan victory over the lesser races or *Untermenschen* (sub-humans). The acquisition of such materials, although reputedly acquired in the name of science and biological research, was also a means of showcasing the conquest of subjugated peoples by the Nazi Aryan race. The Nazi obsession with Aryanism evolved around the racial and biological superiority ethos as interpreted not only by Adolf Hitler himself, but also endorsed by many physicians and geneticists within the German medical community as a whole. This was despite the fact that the people referred to as 'the Aryans' in ancient human history were an ethnoculturally self-designated group of indo-Iranians, also encompassing people of India, who were not geographically, culturally or genetically related to the Germans, ancient or modern.

Nazi physical and biological stereotyping espoused its own entirely false set of Aryan ideals, which of course were in keeping with its racial and political ideology. Furthermore, many German physicians and scientists supported racial hygiene theories well in advance of the Nazis' rise to power in the 1930s. From 1933 onwards they embraced the Nazi view of biology and heredity. This not only endeared these individuals to the regime itself, but also opened new career avenues with additional funding for research. The Aryan race philosophy so beloved of Hitler and other leading Nazis, including many within the medical community, was of course pure fantasy, as there has never been an 'Aryan race' in the course of human evolution. The Nazi interpretation of Aryanism was built around ideas of pure Germanic blood lines, blond hair and blue eyes, and for males a strong appearance and physical strength. Females too should possess blonde hair and blue eyes and be raised under a harsh physical regime in order to remain in optimum health, specifically for childbearing duties.

It is worth noting that societies comprising many individuals with the physiological characteristics of blonde hair and blue eyes resided in particular geographical areas of Europe including northern France, northern Germany, Scandinavia, Denmark, Norway and Sweden. The Nazis considered these people to possess Aryan heritage, and viewed them as racially and biologically valuable. Hitler even thought of the English as fellow Anglo-Saxons, and thus part of the exclusive Aryan club. Evolutionary evidence suggests that these traits became common in Nordic societies during the last Ice Age, as a result of 'sexual selection'. The term sexual selection applies to the principle of a social evolution based around an arbitrary preference for a particular trait in the opposite sex. This in turn creates sexual selection as one sex is driving the evolution of a trait in the other sex. Of course, much research and debate has arisen as a result of this theory, which may sound a little farfetched, but is perfectly feasible when one considers the sexual preferences displayed by both men and women in society today. How many modern men and women would state a preference for a good-looking male or female with blonde hair and blue eyes?

Hitler and the Nazis considered that Jews, Gypsies and Negroes, along with the people of Russia and eastern Europe, fell into the category of *Untermenschen*, or sub-humans, and that they were much less desirable elements of humanity who existed merely to serve as slaves for the superior races. However, during the German invasion of Poland and other territories in eastern Europe, any children deemed suitable for Germanization – that is, with blonde hair and blue eyes – were

6   The Nazi and Japanese Human Experimentation Programmes

taken from their families and placed in the care of German families to be raised as Germans. These children were subject to thorough medical examination, and their facial features, such as the nose, chin, forehead, ears and spacing of the eyes were examined and measured. If the facial features were out of proportion to the Nazi doctrines of the physical aesthetic – i.e. the nose, ears, or forehead were too large or pronounced – the child could still be rejected and would face almost certain death in one of the camps.

The Nazi obsession with the physiological characteristics of the different races within Europe mirrors the fascination with phrenology, as developed by the German physician Franz Joseph Gall in 1796. Phrenology was a pseudoscience that involved the measurement of bumps on the human skull as a means of determining the mental traits of an individual. Phrenology, despite being popular, was by the 1840s regarded with contempt by many professional physicians and soon became thought of as quack medicine. During the early part of the twentieth century phrenology enjoyed a brief resurgence of popularity due in part to the increase in medical studies conducted into human evolution, criminology and anthropology. While there is no hard evidence to suggest that phrenology served to influence the Nazi racial sciences, there are some similarities which cannot be completely ignored. Only recently a wooden chest containing medical instruments, which included a head-measuring device of the type used in the practice of phrenology, was discovered in Argentina with a hoard of Second World War Nazi artefacts.

The exceptions to those young children regarded as suitable for Germanization were those with what was said to have been 'the tainted blood of Jewish ancestry'. Jewish children, however Aryan their appearance, were exempt from this process and were sent to the extermination camps with all other Jews. Such was the perceived threat posed by Jewry to the Nazis that they insisted that no Jew should be permitted to survive under the Third Reich. In Hitler's deluded and twisted thinking he saw himself as some form of self-proclaimed messiah, whose duty it was to erase from the world the undesirable races, the physically and mentally inept, and those he termed the interbred, through some form of divine apocalypse. It is frightening how such a vile philosophy could be so readily embraced by such a highly developed and intelligent modern society as existed in Germany, or how the political force of just one man could convince a society that they were the embodiment of an Aryan master race whose divine duty it was to conquer the world through the destruction of others.

As fantastical as all of the racial rhetoric was, many followed willingly and while the elders should have known better, the youth were brainwashed from their earliest years of education to follow the political and social lines of the Nazi Party. Some understanding of this whole concept goes some way to explaining the attitude of those committed Nazis whose task it was to destroy human life without compassion or conscience, and why so little value was placed upon the lives of those considered racially or biologically inferior.

As the Third Reich embarked upon its mission of conquest, it rounded up thousands of condemned Jews, gypsies and individuals during the invasion of the eastern territories. These individuals would be either executed upon arrival at the many death camps of Nazi-occupied Europe, or worked to death. Many would perish from a combination of harsh living conditions, brutal treatment and lack of adequate food, water and medical attention. Some unfortunate souls were selected to serve as human guinea pigs for all manner of experimentation carried out in the name of Nazi medical science. These experiments were many and varied and we will look at the case studies of some of them, as well as the individuals who perpetrated them. It seems almost obscene, but many of those involved in the Nazi medical experiments developed a strong affection for some of their helpless subjects. Perhaps a good example is Josef Mengele and his twins. In a few of these cases these more cherished victims fared far better than others and were able to survive until their liberation. Nonetheless, the fine line between what one might view as bona fide medical research and that which

8   The Nazi and Japanese Human Experimentation Programmes

can only be described as medical/surgical torture became increasingly blurred as those in the Axis hierarchy sought to play God with their helpless victims.

Elsa Lanneberger was a young medical student at a time when tumultuous events overtook Germany as a country and its society.

'The whole sphere of the German medical profession began to steadily change especially from 1929 following the Wall Street Crash. Many of the developed nations were badly affected, Germany even more so, as Germany was still having to pay large sums of money in reparations for the First World War. I was able to continue my studies largely unaffected despite the medical profession being hit as hard as any other at that time. It was only when Hitler gained power in 1933 that Jewish doctors and surgeons were immediately informed, they would no longer be able to practice medicine. Failure to heed the warnings would mean arrest and imprisonment. Initially, this however unfortunate if morally wrong stance probably did not cause many German medical students too much concern either. We thought well, we can carry on, but such romantic notions were somewhat premature. I myself was told that under the new government proposals for the German medical profession all women studying medicine to become doctors and/or hospital surgeons were to cease their studies with immediate effect. Yes, it was totally preposterous and was something that would have a detrimental effect upon the German health profession as a whole. This new law was by no means anything new as discriminatory laws were being introduced on a daily basis once Herr Hitler had gained power. Some of these clearly discriminatory laws would affect not only Jews but many Germans too. My parents were furious when they heard about it. My father in particular raged "who the hell is Hitler to say my daughter who has spent years at study can no longer finish her studies to become a doctor? Has this man lost his senses."

My mother pleaded for calm and reminded father that if anyone overheard him, we could all face arrest and then where would we be? We sat down and tried to find a means as to how I might be able to continue my studies. I was eighteen years of age, and it was 1938, one year away from the Second World War breaking out in Europe. One proposal my father suggested was that I leave Germany and go to France, England, or America. I had never been out of Germany before, and the thought was daunting but at the same time it was something to consider. I spoke English and French reasonably well so there would be no language barriers as such. As I couldn't study anymore in the professional context I continued at home as best I could by going over all of study essays and going through my books of course. I think it was two weeks after I was informed that I could no longer study medicine that the authorities actually came to our home and asked that I hand over all of the printed textbooks I had used or referred to for my work and studies. I didn't wish to argue with them as they looked in no mood for any messing around, so I did as they asked and handed over the books and manuals. That was it after that and they just left. It hadn't occurred to me at that moment that some of the medical texts I had been using for my studies had been prepared by Jewish-born physicians. Apparently, many medical students including male ones had their textbooks confiscated. The males were told new ones would be issued in due course once all of the material had undergone review by the state. I later learned all of the medical texts written by Jewish authors had been burned. It was at that point my father again brought up the prospect of me leaving Germany to study abroad. It was a hard decision as I wanted to remain in Germany, as all my family and friends were here but in order to achieve my career goals it would not be possible to stay in the country I had loved up until that point in time. My father made arrangements for me to travel to America where he had many contacts plus two

10 The Nazi and Japanese Human Experimentation Programmes

distant cousins living in New York. He told me I would be alright if I went there, and I could write and let them know how I was getting on. We didn't really consider the prospect that war was looming despite it being obvious in many ways or the possible consequences this would have on us as a family and me being a German national in an 'enemy country'. I took my father's advice, and in the July of 1938 packed some things and within two weeks I was arriving in America by ocean liner. My father's relatives were waiting for me, and I remember them holding up these boards with my name on in big letters saying, "Hello Elsa, welcome to America"! I never imagined at that point in time that it would be six years later when I would be returning to Germany with an American mobile medical unit where I would be treating wounded American and German soldiers in the aftermath of the failed German Ardennes offensive or Battle of the Bulge as it was known. It would also be in the wake of the disastrous war Germany had waged across the European continent that I would learn how the medical and surgical professions in Germany had been party to the horrific abuses of innocent human beings in the name of medical experimentation. I would encounter and treat some of these unfortunate tortured souls myself and it made me almost physically sick to call myself a German.'

With so many German women ousted from prospective medical careers in the years following Hitler's seizure of power in 1933, the profession became dominated by men to an even greater extent. Some women, including those who would later be affiliated with the SS, working alongside the likes of Josef Mengele in the hell holes such as Auschwitz, continued with their so-called medical careers, but there were nowhere near the numbers of females within the medical profession as there were prior to Hitler's ascension to power. Most young German male students who aimed to become military or civilian doctors or surgeons had to have been members of the compulsory *Hitler Jugend* (Hitler

A Divine Apocalypse 11

Youth) movement. Any student who avoided Hitler Youth membership, or who fell out of the Hitler Youth for any reason, could be prevented by the Nazi authorities from enrolling in university education. The Nazis, through the new education system, Hitler Youth and *Bund Deutscher Madel* (League of German Maidens), redefined the medical ethos, which had previously embraced all of those in need. The new Nazi regime not only expelled Jewish doctors, nurses and surgeons from their various clinical professions, but also set out to deny Jews and others construed as belonging to a lesser race even the most basic everyday medical care. It was education through racism and persecution and a deliberate attempt at hardening the German consciousness in readiness for the horrors which were to come.

There are two particular aspects which require understanding when examining the specific forms of medical research conducted upon live human beings throughout the Nazi era. The first is the totalitarian political system espoused by the National Socialist regime and the broader paradigm of Nazi racial hygiene, something which did not occur exclusively as a result of the Nazi political system, but rather of a social movement drawing upon concepts created by the understanding of contemporary biology, the origins of which preceded the ascension of the Nazi Party by more than twenty years. The autocratic political system, and the programme of racial hygiene, reinforced each other as concepts, thus contributing to specific questions to be addressed by the medical sciences, all within a setting where no ethical or legal regulations were in place. The combination of these factors provided the conditions for medical experimentation on live human beings to be undertaken, where previously it would not have been deemed possible. The Nazi German equivalent of the study of eugenics known as *Rassenhygiene* or 'racial hygiene' was viewed as an applied science founded upon the laws of genetics and seen as an essential element in improving the health of the Nazi German nation. It was hoped that through the application of science a long-term solution would be found to prevent defects in human genetic material, which in turn would complement

12 The Nazi and Japanese Human Experimentation Programmes

individual hygiene. Pivotal to the Nazi racial hygiene ethos was the concept that humans live and behave as they do by virtue of their biological constitution, and ultimately their genes. The Nazi medical institutions were keen to legitimise their health and racial policies, in particular the implementation of the Nazi sterilisation law 'for the prevention of genetically diseased offspring'. This law, implemented on 14 July 1933, meant that any German national within the Reich territory suffering from any physical or mental disability assumed to be a hereditary condition could be subject to forced sterilisation. These disabilities included deafness, schizophrenia, epilepsy, blindness, severe deformity and even severe alcohol addiction. This law was seen as a logical step towards the protection of the racial integrity of the future German Reich. Many disabled members of Nazi society, even if totally sound of mind, were subject to forced sterilisation and/or abortion. Many would later be murdered by German medical professionals under cover of the ruthless Nazi T4 Euthanasia programme, in which an estimated 200,000 disabled children and adults were murdered in purpose-built gas chambers. Lunatic asylums were also rapidly vacated using the T4 Euthanasia programme, but not before some of these unfortunate patients were selected to undergo horrifying so-called 'medical experiments'. Many of those labelled as lunatics or imbeciles within the asylum system were spared sterilisation but were instead simply murdered and their corpses incinerated. Some of the bodies had internal organs such as their brains removed for medical study prior to their incineration. The organs were removed and placed in large glass vessels filled either with alcohol (60%) or Formalin (an aqueous solution of formaldehyde). Both methods of preservation inhibited the process of necrosis in human organs and tissue taken for medical research purposes. In many respects medical research into hereditary diseases, deformity, mental illness and disability experienced a huge resurgence of study under the Nazi regime. Many doctors and surgeons in Nazi Germany thus pursued their disciplines in much the same way as a philatelist would collect stamps. It was in every respect a licence

A Divine Apocalypse 13

allowing the wholesale abuse of not only thousands of human beings, but the medical system itself.

The Hitler Youth organisation for Nazi Germany's children served not only as a tool with which to indoctrinate young Germans in the political and social beliefs of the Nazi regime, but also to weed out any children considered to be unfit Aryans. The categorisation of an unfit Aryan was simple. Any child discovered to be suffering from any debilitating physical or mental defects would be discovered through the Hitler Youth medical, physical and academic selection process. The Hitler Youth would only select the physically able and mentally proficient to join its ranks. Any individual falling outside of the expected criteria would find him or herself under very close scrutiny, not only from the state, but also from their Hitler Youth colleagues. To illustrate this ruthless process of physical and mental selection I present some examples that were obtained from former members of both the female and male Hitler Youth organisations.

Anna Dann, who had been a member of the girls' Hitler Youth, the *Bund Deutscher Madel* (BDM), recalled how some girls struggled with the physical and mental expectations of them within the BDM, and the sinister consequences which inevitably followed. Anna recalled:

'There were not many young girls who could not make the grade and gain membership into the movement. So, it is easy for me to remember those who could not and what became of them. There was a girl who seemed to perform very well in the mental aspects of the Hitler Youth, yet she struggled when it came to the more important physical side of things. There was a lot of running, medicine ball throwing, gymnastics and swimming involved and yes it was very intense and time penalties were placed on these tasks which had to be completed within an allotted time. The girl in question would rapidly tire and begin to fight for breath in the physical events which were considered essential. In cross country running events she fell so far behind the leaders

14   The Nazi and Japanese Human Experimentation Programmes

of our troop would scold her and call her a weakling and to get a move on. It became obvious that she was very physically unfit for some reason. A doctor was called to examine her lungs and it was discovered she was suffering with some form of asthma. The consequences of this were that the doctor insisted her family were also subject to a thorough medical examination. In the event the girl in question I mention was sent to one of the clinics to be sterilized. Yes, they sterilized her, and she was only fifteen years of age. Her father and mother protested, and I heard that as a punishment both her parents were sterilized too. They made no secret that anyone weak or inept would not be acceptable to the new Germany. Even if we carried an injury due to any of our sporting activities, we did not show any pain or discomfort as we were scared, they might do the same to us. It made you push through any pain barriers you might have had, just ignore it and the pain will go in time.'

Kurt Busche, a former Hitler Youth member from Heidelberg, recalls an instance which he remembers as 'the Fat Kid'.

'When the Hitler Youth became compulsory for us all to join, they didn't just throw a uniform and badge at you. No, it was a very stringent process of selection much like that employed by our armed forces at the time. The Hitler Youth had these doctors many of which were associated with the SS as these doctors did not want any child showing signs of any hereditary diseases both of a mental or physical nature. We had all sorts of physical tests, and they would examine you all over from head to toe making personal notes about you as they did. I would say I was average height and weight, and I was a fit young lad as I had hiked, cycled, run and swam before I had joined the Hitler Youth, I was certainly one of those lads who was never inside come summer or winter and I loved the outdoors and being with my friends doing what young lads always do. We climbed trees had running and swimming races with one another, so we were already pretty competitive, and the Hitler Youth hones this competitive spirit in us. I recall having gone through the selection process being introduced to the leader of our district group. He was a tall kid with blonde hair blue eyes and very masculine indeed. He would puff out his chest and bark at you like a sergeant. He just told us new members "it is good that you are not late joining the party, there is no jelly and ice cream here, we do not want mummy's boys, weaklings or non-patriots and we don't want queers (homosexuals). We will find out all we need to know about you, if you work hard and we find you acceptable you will become a brother to every other boy here."

I recall this big lad turning up, I say big he was not big in the sense of being tall or anything he was rather big around the waist. Although he had passed entry inspections the group leader was determined that the physical regimen would make him lose weight. It turned out to be hopeless this lad couldn't run and of course all the other boys ridiculed him for this. He couldn't climb either, yet he swam pretty good. Overall, his performance was below par, and they classed him as physically inept which was very bad for a young male in Hitler's Germany. I remember this kid being mocked by not only the leader but the other boys too. They would say to him "look at you – you are fat just like a Jew" and they would nickname him "Fat Kid". He was removed and we did not see him again and we would hear all sorts of rumours but most of these rumours could never be confirmed. I assumed they sent him to work somewhere out of the way maybe in a factory or something. The idea was that boys would be honed towards military service. The Hitler Youth was much like a young boy's army as it was training us towards military service.'

16 The Nazi and Japanese Human Experimentation Programmes

Antionette Hilbe's recollection is particularly disturbing, involving the youngest of her three brothers, named Artur.

'Artur was my youngest brother, and he was born in 1932. When Artur was born there was no immediate indication that anything was wrong with him. He looked fine but as he grew older, we soon realised that he had a few learning problems. Mother and father worked very hard with him at home when he was little in the hope that he would be alright once schooling began. The Nazis had been in total power of Germany a year and we were beginning to hear of the things they were proposing both socially and politically. All the talk about how the youth were the future and that they must be strong, resilient and ruthless in every pursuit. The boys were the main focus of the Nazi regime. They would be the soldiers of the future and they had to educated and physically fit. We were not stupid, and we understood that we were going to face some serious problems with Artur. It would not be us that would have any problem with Artur as we loved him dearly, but we knew trouble would come once Artur entered first school. My mother tried to hold out for as long as she could and school Artur at home, but this drew the attention of the authorities who wanted to know why Artur was not joining the community. We knew there was no way he would ever excel at either school or the Hitler Youth and after a bad day at the local school I remember these men came to visit our parents. They insisted on seeing and talking with Artur and when they sat him down, they began asking him questions like "Why did you mess yourself today Artur"? "Do you know how you should address your teacher"? "Do you know that this behaviour is unfitting of a German"? Then they would ask him "Can you spell imbecile"? "Can you count how many fingers I am holding up Artur"? Just horrible questions really and they knew he was not like the other boys, and we just hoped they would let mother school him at home and leave him alone but no he was on the radar now as being mentally unfit, backward or an imbecile as they would say. We were all summoned for medical examinations which were humiliating. The authorities wanted to ensure we kids were not in possession of defective genes as they put it. I myself was in a room with two doctors one female one male and they told me to remove my clothing before examining me like an animal at a show. They took blood and saliva samples from me and examined every part of my body, and it was very intrusive, and I didn't like it. My birth records were scrutinized along with those of my elder brothers before all of our documents were given an official stamp of clearance from the doctors. They did the same with Artur and my parents were not permitted to be with him throughout his examination which did not go well. The doctors concluded that Artur should be admitted to one of the specialist clinics where he could undergo further tests and examinations to ascertain how he became defective while we other siblings were fine. We returned home and I recall a few days later after I came home from school Artur was not at home. My mother was sat at the kitchen table with her head in her hands weeping. I asked her "Mother what's wrong, where's Artur"? Mother just blurted out "He has gone, they have taken him to one of their clinics and I don't know even know where it is or when I can go to see him, they have told me nothing". Over the weeks that followed my parents received letters informing them that Artur was fine and that they were conducting tests which would take time and that we should not worry about him. It all sounded very sinister to me even at that young age that I was. The final letter from the authorities arrived two months later and this typed document informed my parents that their dear Artur had contracted measles while at the hospital and had died and to ensure that the outbreak was contained it was deemed necessary to cremate the bodies of those who had died straightaway. So, there was no body, no grave for us to visit there was nothing at all. It was at that point I possessed nothing but loathing for Hitler and his Nazis. Yet Artur was not the only one who had been found to be mentally defective and taken away and later the family told they had died of disease while in the care of the hospitals. It was all a lie as they were systematically killing the mentally and physically disabled all over Germany. The problem was there was no document trail as when a patient as they called them expired, they were cremated, and their files burned. They had even retained Artur's birth certificate, and my parents never had this returned to them. The letter informing them of Artur's death due to measles was thrown into the fire by my father in a fit of rage so even after the war we could not find a trail back to those responsible and report them. This was your Nazi Germany, anyone not found to fit their perfect Aryan physiological ideals for the future were taken away and euthanized and the mentally and physically infirm were considered a burden upon the state as they would cost the state more money than a healthy German and tie down medical resources which would be better employed elsewhere than the treating of these unfit Aryans as they were categorised'.

Chapter 3

Human Guinea Pigs

Many might think that the outbreak of the Second World War in September 1939, triggered by the German invasion of Poland, was when the proposal for Nazi concentration camps was conceived. However, the first camps had been established as early as March 1933 in the wake of Adolf Hitler being appointed Chancellor of Germany. The *Sturmabteilung* (Storm Troopers) or *Braunhemden* (Brown Shirts), also known simply as the SA, had been created as a kind of security force which served the fledgling Nazi Party well throughout its tumultuous early years. Yet the following year, between 30 June and 2 July 1934, the SA was brutally disbanded in what has since become infamous as 'The Night of the Long Knives'. Many of the seemingly loyal SA leadership, including Ernst Rohm, were arrested and executed. The purge of the SA was yet another component in the Nazi consolidation of power and was also seen as a preventative measure against an alleged imminent SA coup. Subsequently the concentration camps were run exclusively by the *Schutzstaffel* or SS (protection squads initially conceived as Adolf Hitler's personal bodyguard) via the *Inspektion der Konzentrationslager* or Concentration Camp Inspectorate (created by Theodor Eicke) and later the SS Main Economic and Administrative Office. Staffing of the concentration camps fell to the SS-TV or SS *Totenkopfverbande* (Death's Head) units. While the death's head symbol became the universal insignia of the SS, including the fighting formations of the *Waffen* (weapon) SS, the SS *Totenkopfverbande* wore this insignia on the right collar tabs of their uniforms in order to distinguish themselves from the other SS formations within the German military.

20 The Nazi and Japanese Human Experimentation Programmes

The SS *Totenkopfverbande* operated as an independent body within the SS, with its own separate command structure. At the outbreak of the Second World War the SS Division *Totenkopf* was formed from members of the SS-TV who staffed the concentration camps. These individuals were committed Nazis with a reputation for violence, cruelty and murder and it is therefore unsurprising that wherever this unit fought in Europe it committed sickening war crimes, as did many other *Waffen* SS fighting units. Although it is not the objective of this work to examine the activities of the SS-TV, it is clear that individuals belonging to these units, both male and female, might have thrived within the concentration camps and willingly assisted in the ghastly activities carried out in these vile institutions. The female SS-TV staff within the concentration camp system were every bit as brutal and sadistic as the males and all complicit in the murder, torture and mutilation carried out in the name of Nazi medical science.

With the concentration camp system well established by the early to mid-1940s, with others either planned or under construction, and the speed of the German rampage through Europe, the camps were soon filled to capacity with unfortunate inmates awaiting their fate. The chief target populations for the proposed Nazi medical experimentation programmes within the camps were the Romani, Sinti, ethnic Poles, Jews and captured Russian prisoners of war. These groups of people were forced into taking part in all manner of medical experiments by the Nazi physicians and their assistants. They were definitely not volunteers, as some Nazi doctors attempted to suggest in the years after the Second World War. The scope of the medical experiments carried out on concentration camp prisoners was vast, ranging from the seemingly miniscule to the absolute extreme. There were some experiments conducted on both male and female prisoners within the camps which were little more than acts of sexual torture, which served no medical research purpose. These acts are covered in more detail in the appropriate section of this book and are sickening to read about. Many of the medical procedures on prisoners were carried out without anaesthesia and without sufficient medical aftercare. As a consequence, the death rate among participants was high, due to both infection and, in some cases, shock. It did not matter to the Nazi physicians that they lost so many prisoners to medical experimentation, as thousands more human guinea pigs were constantly arriving in railway cattle trucks from the East. Those who survived suffered physical trauma, disfigurement, mutilation and permanent disability. They were also psychologically scarred, with some victims left in such unbearable mental agony that despite surviving their ordeal they would later take their own lives after their liberation. Just how many victims of Nazi medical experimentation died by suicide is not entirely clear. Even those who underwent treatment after the war in an attempt to repair the physical damage done to their bodies often died well before old age due to the severity of their conditions and irreversible tissue, bone, nerve and organ damage. It is one of the darkest chapters of recent human history.

Chapter 4

The Nazi Medical Experiments

The Nazi programme of human medical experiments was vast, with a great many individuals involved in day-to-day operations. It would be impossible to examine each and every method of medical experimentation used by the Nazi doctors during the Second World War, and to list the individual perpetrators involved. Thus I present here some examples of the types of experiments conducted, with a brief explanation and data on the individuals involved where these details are known.

In the Nazi German view, perhaps the most important sector of the Nazi human medical experimentation programme was that conceived to assist the German military in combat situations, the creation of more effective weaponry, and the treatment and recovery of wounded German military personnel in combat.

SS *Obersturmbannfuhrer* (Lieutenant Colonel) Eduard Wirths, born on 4 September 1909 at Geroldshausen, in the German Empire, was the chief SS doctor (SS-*Standortarzt*) at the infamous Auschwitz concentration camp in Poland from September 1942 to January 1945. Wirths was given formal responsibility for all activities in a medical/surgical context at Auschwitz, which included work undertaken not only by himself, but also by his team of twenty SS doctors present in the camp, including Josef Mengele, Horst Schumann and Carl Clauberg. Wirths, a committed Nazi, was significantly immersed in Nazi ideology in three crucial spheres: (a) the claim of revitalizing the German race and its peoples, (b) the biomedical path to the revitalization via the purification of genes and racial bloodlines, and (c) the focus on the Jewish race as a threat to this system of renewal. Wirths, it seems, was a somewhat contradictory character. Generally, he was remembered favourably by both the SS doctors whom he presided over and also the prisoners who had contact with him. It was, however, Wirths who recommended Dr Josef Mengele for promotion in the camp in August 1944 and spoke highly of him, concluding that he was:

'an open, honest, firm and absolutely dependable character, with magnificent intellectual and physical talents, of the discretion, perseverance, and energy with which he has fulfilled every task and shown himself equal to every situation of his valuable contribution to anthropological science by making use of the scientific materials available to him, of his absolute ideological firmness and faultless conduct as an SS officer and personal qualities as free, unrestrained, persuasive, and lively discourse that rendered him especially dear to his comrades'.

That is quite some reference for such a monster as Dr Mengele. Yet on Christmas Day 1943 Wirths received a Christmas card from a political prisoner which contained the following message written inside: 'In the past year you have here the lives of 93,000 people. We do not have the right to tell you, our wishes. But we wish for ourselves that you stay here in the coming year'. The card was signed 'Langbein – one speaking for the prisoners of Auschwitz'. The figure of 93,000 was the reduction in the mortality rate from typhus in the year since Wirths's arrival at the Auschwitz camp. Prevention of deaths from typhus by no means excuses Wirths from the criminal assaults on innocent human beings that also took place on his watch, and he should be seen as every bit as complicit in these crimes as Mengele and the others.

Sterilization and fertility experiments

The Nazi law for the Prevention of Genetically Defective Progeny was introduced in Nazi Germany on 14 July 1933. This gave the Nazi

24   The Nazi and Japanese Human Experimentation Programmes

authorities the legal power to carry out involuntary mass sterilization, including of any persons with diseases deemed to be hereditary, such as mental illness, schizophrenia, alcohol abuse, insanity, blindness, deafness, and physical deformities or disability. The law was conceived to protect and encourage the advancement of the proposed German Aryan race. One per cent of the population aged between seventeen and twenty-four was sterilized through this programme within two years of its implementation; after four years some 300,000 citizens were forcibly sterilized in what had become a highly organized clinical programme. From March 1941 to around January 1945 sterilization experiments were carried out at Auschwitz, Ravensbruck (a women's camp) and other institutions under the direction of Carl Clauberg.

Carl Clauberg, born on 28 September 1898 in Wupperhof, German Empire, had served as an infantryman in the First World War. At the war's end in 1918 he went on to study medicine, reaching the rank of chief doctor at the Kiel University gynaecological clinic. Clauberg joined the Nazi Party in 1933, later being appointed associate professor of gynaecology at the University of Konigsberg. Clauberg's research focussed on female fertility hormones (particularly progesterone) and their application as infertility treatments. He gained a Habilitation (highest University degree) for this work in 1937. Clauberg received the rank of SS-*Gruppenfuhrer* of the SS Reserve.

Clauberg was able to join the Nazi sterilization programme thanks to a recommendation from SS chief Heinrich Himmler, who had heard of him through a colleague whose wife Clauberg had treated. This high-level endorsement from Himmler allowed Clauberg to carry out all manner of sterilization experiments, mostly on women, starting in 1942 when he began his work at the Auschwitz concentration camp. Clauberg's laboratory was located in Block 10, situated within the main camp. He aimed to find the simplest and cheapest method by which to sterilize women. Clauberg's methods were both crude and extremely painful, as they were carried out without any anaesthesia being administered. One such method was to inject formaldehyde

The Nazi Medical Experiments   25

directly into a woman's uterus. Most of the victims of this procedure were Romani and Jewish women. Many suffered severe and permanent damage and infection, and it is reported that Clauberg was responsible for carrying out this procedure on at least 700 women, of whom a large proportion died as a result. Himmler was eager to discover how much time it might take to sterilize 1,000 Jewish women using the method of formaldehyde injection. Clauberg replied that a single doctor with ten assistants should be able to conduct the sterilization of a few hundred, or even a few thousand, Jews in just one day.

Clauberg was particularly interested in experimenting on women aged twenty to forty who had already given birth. Prior to any procedure Clauberg would X-ray his subject to ensure that there was no obstruction to the ovaries. Over the course of three to five sessions, he would inject the woman's cervix with the intention of blocking the fallopian tubes. If any of the women questioned or attempted to refuse the procedure they would be classified as unfit test subjects and sent away to be killed in the gas chambers. Clauberg used solutions such as iodine and silver nitrate in his injections, and it was observed that these caused side effects such as vaginal bleeding, severe abdominal pain and cervical cancer. Therefore, Clauberg surmised that radiation treatment would provide the best method of sterilization. This radiation treatment was administered via X-ray equipment. Specific doses of exposure to radiation destroyed a person's ability to produce either ova or sperm, and in many instances this treatment was administered through deception and without the subject's knowledge. Female subjects received X-ray doses to their abdomen, while male subjects received the same dosage to their genitals for abnormally long periods of time in order to render the subject infertile. After these experiments were completed, the subjects' reproductive organs were surgically removed without anaesthesia and the specimens were then taken for laboratory analysis by Clauberg and his colleagues.

Physically, Clauberg was of short, squat-faced appearance and wore circular spectacles – hardly a fine representation of Hitler's proposed

26　The Nazi and Japanese Human Experimentation Programmes

Aryan race. There were many more doctors like him. For example, an Austrian Nazi doctor named Hermann Stieve specifically focussed on the female reproductive system. He claimed to be able to tell women their date of death in advance, and he would evaluate how their psychological distress would affect their menstrual cycles. After they were murdered, Stieve would dissect and examine their reproductive organs. Some of his victims were raped after they were told the date they would be killed so he could study the path of sperm through their reproductive systems. It beggars belief that such things could happen, but the evidence is clear.

Mustard gas experiments

There were various periods between September 1939 and April 1945 when experiments were conducted at the Sachsenhausen and Natzweiler concentration camps to investigate the most effective methods of treating wounds caused by mustard gas. Mustard gas, or sulphur mustard, is any of several chemical compounds comprised of the chemical makeup SCH_2CH_2C1. In a wider context, compounds with the substituent SCH_2CH_2X and NCH_2CH_2X are known as sulphur mustards and nitrogen mustards (X=Cl, Br), respectively. These compounds are powerful alkylating agents, capable of interfering with numerous biological processes. Also often referred to as mustard agents, this group of chemical compounds are notorious cytotoxic and blister agents. Those exposed to mustard gas develop large painful fluid filled blisters. These blisters usually form on any tissues that have been exposed to the gas and can also infect the lungs leading to further medical complications within the respiratory system and body in general. Death from exposure to mustard gas depends largely upon the amount of gas ingested by an individual yet it is certainly neither quick nor merciful. Mustard gas as a general term is a technically incorrect description. These chemicals once released are not actually released in a gas form as we understand it but more of a fine mist comprising

The Nazi Medical Experiments   27

liquid droplets much like the moisture experienced in foggy conditions. Mustard gases react with human DNA, which in turn interferes with cellular division, which can lead to mutations. The toxicity of mustard gas cannot be emphasized enough here. It is a highly carcinogenic agent, and anyone deliberately exposed to it without the necessary full body, face and head protection will experience the following symptoms soon, or almost instantly following exposure.

Within twenty-four hours of exposure the victim will experience intense itching coupled with skin irritation. Pus-filled blisters start to form wherever the agent has made contact with unprotected skin. These blisters are actually burns caused by the chemical and are extremely debilitating. Normal clothing does not guarantee protection against mustard gas as the vapour easily penetrates fabrics such as wool or cotton. If the subject's eyes are exposed to the gas the eyes soon become very sore, starting with conjunctivitis, after which the eyelids swell, resulting in temporary blindness. Extreme ocular exposure to the gas can cause permanent blindness. It was not uncommon for victims of mustard gas exposure to suffer bleeding within the respiratory system, damaging mucous membranes and causing pulmonary oedema. Depending upon the level of mustard gas exposure burns can vary between first and second degree, though they can be every bit as severe, disfiguring, and dangerous as third-degree burns. Burns that cover more than 50 per cent of the victim's skin often prove fatal, with death occurring within days or weeks. Mild exposure to mustard gas, though unlikely to prove fatal, nonetheless requires the victim to receive lengthy periods of medical treatment and convalescence before recovery is complete.

In the concentration camps helpless prisoners were placed in what were effectively gas chambers, albeit on a smaller scale, with glass vision ports so that the effects of the gas could be observed. In the Nazi human experimentation tests mustard gas was administered by doctors wearing protective clothing and gas masks. The gas was either administered in patches which were then attached to the skin, or a measured dose of the mustard gas was contained within a glass phial

28   The Nazi and Japanese Human Experimentation Programmes

which would then be broken to release a cloud of the gas. Eyewitness accounts of these experiments are rare, but I was able to obtain one account from a Herr Pasch, who interviewed numerous former Polish concentration camp prisoners while compiling material for a proposed book in 1997. The following account of a typical mustard gas exposure experiment was given during an interview that same year with Alexei Kowalczyk, who was a prisoner in the Sachsenhausen concentration camp in 1943.

'I was taken into a room which looked like a prison cell, there were no windows to the outside just a light and a large glass viewing window in the wall. The door into this room was heavy like a prison door and there was a chair directly opposite the large glass viewing window in the room. The chair was bolted to the floor to prevent it from moving. It looked like an execution chair, an electric chair, that's what it looked like as there were head, arm and leg straps on the chair. I thought that they were going to electrocute me and was resigned to the fact that I was going to be dead probably in a few minutes. I was instructed to remove all of my clothing which was not much, just the normal striped jacket and trousers what we all had to wear. They did not tell me anything other than to sit down in the chair. Once I had sat down, they strapped me to it so I could not move at all. The door to the room was closed and the same doctors then joined others at the viewing window looking directly at me. They were very casual and were smiling to one another and talking. Yes, I was very frightened as I did not know what was going to happen. I thought that they couldn't possibly electrocute me as I could see no electrical wiring on the chair I was strapped into. After what must have been a couple of minutes a hatch in the wall was opened and what looked to be a round glass object was forcibly thrown through and the hatch closed. As the glass shattered on the floor a fine mist was released into the room, immediately my eyes began to sting to the point they watered, and I could not see clearly. I knew I was being gassed but with what I had no idea, due to my fear I was breathing very heavily but tried to breathe through my nose to minimise taking in whatever this stuff was. I was aware of the door to the room opening and being unstrapped from the chair and rapidly being dragged out and into what must have been another room where I was left for several hours or so. My eyes were very sore and swollen and my skin had begun to itch so badly that I scratched at myself, but no matter how hard I scratched I could not relieve the itching. I was aware of blisters forming on my skin and many of these broke open as I scratched making the wounds even more sore. My breathing was very painful, and I coughed up a lot of bile which caused really bad pain in my chest. My eyes had closed due to the effects of whatever that stuff was as I did not know it was mustard gas at that time. They came back and placed me in a room where I was hosed down with cold water like an animal for several minutes. I was aware of being examined medically in the days afterwards and given various treatments much like a rat in some laboratory. They never did this to me again but the effects of what I later discovered was due to mustard gas exposure remained with me and I still suffer from poor health today as a result.'

Bone, muscle, and nerve transplantation experiments

From around September 1942 to December 1943 a series of experiments were carried out at the Ravensbruck concentration camp, with the aim of benefiting the German armed forces. The experiments focussed on the study of bone, muscle and nerve generation, and bone transplantation from one human subject to another. During the course of these experiments victims had bones, muscle and nerve tissues removed from various areas of their anatomy without any anaesthesia being administered beforehand.

30   The Nazi and Japanese Human Experimentation Programmes

One survivor of these experiments was a young Polish girl named Jadwiga Kaminska. She recalled the operations conducted upon her body:

'I was operated on twice, on both occasions they operated on my legs though I had no knowledge of what exactly they were doing to me. Both times I was in extreme pain throughout and after the procedures developing post-operative fever on both occasions. I was given no aftercare at all after these procedures were finished. My legs began to ooze pus after these procedures and continued to do so for some months afterwards. They told me I was being operated on simply because I was a "young girl and a Polish patriot".'

Experiments were also carried out in which prisoners were given injections of bacteria into their bone marrow. These extremely painful procedures were carried out to study the effectiveness of new drugs being developed for use on the battlefields, drugs which in turn might save more German lives. Even if these procedures proved successful, many of those who survived suffered some form of permanent disfigurement. Olga Horrowitz, who was a nineteen-year-old Polish girl at Auschwitz, recalled that in February 1943 she was taken to a surgical block at the camp where doctors told her to remove her clothing before strapping her down on to a white operating table. Olga recalled what happened next:

'They strapped me down by my wrists with leather restraints which were attached to the sides of the table, they did this so as my arms were strapped down to the side of my body. Then they secured leather straps around my ankles, and I remember thinking the metal buckles on the straps were very cold against my skin. I began to tremble as I was very frightened about what they were going to do with me. The Germans all wore white surgical masks over their faces so I could not distinguish who they were or one from the

The Nazi Medical Experiments   31

other. One told me to remain relaxed and still in a reassuring tone while another was sterner and told me to stop shaking and try to keep still. They had this small table on wheels with metal dishes containing what looked like surgical tools. One of the Germans took one of the tools from one of the metal dishes and turned to the area of my shin bone. For a moment I felt nothing then there was this very sharp stinging pain. I couldn't see very clearly what he was doing to my leg as a leather strap placed around my throat prevented me from positioning my head so as I could see. All I could see was this German drawing his arm back as if he were tracing a line, the pain began to increase and became so intense that I tried to struggle and I began shouting at them "what are you doing, please don't hurt me, why are you hurting me, please stop". I begged them and the pain was so intense in my leg that my body went into a cold sweat, I could feel the sweat on my skin but it was cold. I must have passed out as I felt my face being slapped around until I came to. How long I had been unconscious I don't know. I was carried out of the room where the surgery had been carried out and placed in a room with other prisoners who had undergone similar procedures. I noticed an incision had been made in my shin, it was five inches long and the skin had been stitched. I lay on the bed moaning with pain and developed a fever over the next few days. The Germans did not give me any medicine all they did was come and look and prod at the wound making notes, other than that it was the other prisoners who gave me help. If it were not for those other prisoners, I would have probably died. One of them a young male also Polish had managed to smuggle some tablets from the SS infirmary he made sure I took two of these small white tablets a day until I had taken them all. I don't know what they were, but the fever steadily decreased and the pus from the wound cleared after a few weeks. The Germans forced me to walk despite the pain I was in, they watched intently as I struggled to walk falling over at times. They stood impassively

32   The Nazi and Japanese Human Experimentation Programmes

watching me taking down notes before laughing and walking away. They sent me back to labour work after a month or so. My leg healed well but has never been the same since and I still get discomfort from what they did to me.'

Olga Horrowitz underwent an operation on her leg after the war to repair damage caused during the procedure carried out by the Nazi doctors. In Olga's words:

'those swine had cut into my bones; my doctor told me it is a miracle I can still walk on that leg. Even after the liberation I was scared as I had heard stories those German doctors had implanted cancerous tissues and body fluids into healthy prisoners to determine if the cancer would take hold and continue to grow within a new host body. It was like something from a horror film that you could never begin to understand unless you had experienced it yourself.'

Concentration camp prisoners selected for surgical procedures also had operations performed upon them in which foreign bodies such as soil, fragments of wood or metal were placed into surgical incisions on their bodies. The wounds were then closed up with sutures and the onset of infection was then carefully observed and various drugs administered to the victim to ascertain which worked best to clear the infection. Some prisoners were deliberately shot in the arms or legs with low-velocity projectiles such as 9mm bullets from a pistol, or high-velocity 7.92mm bullets from an army rifle. The damage to bone and tissues was then examined as the wound area was dissected in an attempt to find the best way of treating the tissue damage and splintered bones. Many of the human guinea pigs selected died from a lack of aftercare, which often led to the onset of blood poisoning. Those lucky enough to recover were often left at least partially crippled by these barbarous acts.

Head injury experiments

Experiments were also carried out in which head injuries were deliberately inflicted upon prisoners. Prisoners were selected and beaten over the head with various implements, often causing blunt trauma injuries. Implements used included heavy sticks and rifle butts. The idea was not to exert sufficient force to kill the prisoner, but to create an injury whereby he or she would survive and be more or less fully aware when operated upon by the Nazi doctors. One such case occurred in Baranowicze, in occupied Poland, in a small building behind the private home of a notable *Sichersdienst* (security service) officer. In this documented case a young boy aged around eleven or twelve was strapped to a chair so he could not move. Placed above his head was a mechanized hammer, which every few seconds came down upon his head. It was reported that the boy was driven insane by the torture.

The prisoners deliberately subjected to head trauma would almost certainly then be killed as they were strapped down on to surgical tables and their skulls opened up with a bone saw to observe the damage caused. Again, these procedures were carried out with no anaesthetic. The idea behind these experiments was to find out how much damage or bleeding to the brain occurred from blows to the head with different objects, and how that damage might be treated. Some victims of forced head trauma were strapped down, and the Nazi doctors would then drill through the skull in the area of trauma, effectively performing a crude form of trepanation to relieve the build-up of blood within the skull, which caused pressure on the brain, and then to observe how the prisoner responded to various treatments administered. Few subjects could survive such a procedure, carried out with no anaesthetic or aftercare. Many of the victims were simply put into the incinerators while still alive, their purpose having been served. Although they often proved instantly fatal, research into gunshot wounds to the head from high-velocity munitions such as 7.7mm, 7.62mm bullets and shrapnel was carried out in a limited capacity in the camps. Such head injuries

34   The Nazi and Japanese Human Experimentation Programmes

were a common problem on the battlefield and were notoriously difficult to treat, due in part to the massive trauma that bullets and shrapnel caused on impact with the soft tissues, skull and brain in both the facial and cranial regions of the head.

Research on this particular subject was somewhat difficult, as most of the records were destroyed along with many others in an attempt to deny that such experiments ever took place. Bodies of those prisoners subject to arbitrary execution – shot in the head at close range by either pistol or rifle – were in some cases examined by the camp doctors in an attempt to gain some understanding of the effects of gunshot wounds to the head. It was soon determined that most gunshot wounds to the head would prove fatal due to the difficulty in treating such wounds and the massive damage to bone and tissues which occurred. Infection was another problem, as debris often became embedded in gunshot and shrapnel wounds. Even cases in which a steel helmet was being worn often proved fatal as fragments of the helmet became secondary projectiles when the bullet struck the metal, propelling broken fragments of steel inwards into the head and brain. A high-velocity bullet, as used in the standard Soviet Mosin Nagant rifle of the time, for example, travelled at a muzzle velocity of between 2,580 feet per second to 2,840 feet per second with muzzle energies (depending on type of projectile) ranging from 2,267 to 2,427-foot pounds. These 7.62mm projectiles created a shockwave at the tip of the bullet and this shockwave alone, prior to the bullet actually impacting the head, was capable of causing grievous damage. Upon entering the head, the bullet would shatter a human skull and the pressure wave created by the bullet as it then passed through the head would cause massive expansion of any tissues in its path. There were of course lucky survivors of gunshot wounds to the head in which the bullet merely grazed the victim's head. These wounds were easily treated through cleaning, suturing and post-operative care. However, there are many cases of concentration camp prisoners being deliberately shot in the legs, in which doctors then examined the damage caused to soft tissue, muscle and bone. The wounds were often

The Nazi Medical Experiments   35

cleaned and sutured and then left for observation, to see if or when any infection might occur in the wound. If infection did occur, rather than being treated it infection was monitored to see how rapidly it would lead to amputation becoming necessary. Any prisoner suffering this would almost certainly be killed afterwards, providing he or she survived the amputation, which in the conditions the prisoners were subject to would have been unlikely. Pre-war experiments into gunshot wounds often used live pigs as subjects.

Stab wound experiments

While bayonet and edged weapon injuries were never going to be as common during the Second World War as they had been during the First World War, research was still carried out into the best methods of treating the sometimes savage wounds caused by stabbing implements. Jewish prisoners at the concentration camps, along with captured Russian prisoners of war, were deliberately stabbed with bayonets and often the wounds were left open so that they would become infected. The varying degrees of infection were monitored and methods of repairing the damage caused were devised. Stab wounds were administered to the legs, arms, stomach and chest. Most bayonet stab injuries occurred around the stomach and chest areas of the body, for the obvious reason that these areas contained the body's vital organs. Most stab wounds to the chest or stomach proved fatal due to the puncturing of organs such as the lungs, liver, intestines and bowels. Nazi German research into stab injuries was minimal, unlike the Japanese Imperial Army, who relished the prospect of using bayonets to kill the enemy.

Freezing experiments

Freezing experiments were also conducted as these were thought to be useful in addressing the problem of hypothermia affecting *Luftwaffe* aircrews operating at high altitudes or having to crash land into the sea.

36   The Nazi and Japanese Human Experimentation Programmes

These particular medical experiments prove that the German *Luftwaffe* (air force) was complicit in the crimes, as the research was carried out not only in their name, but also by members of the *Luftwaffe* itself, albeit within the concentration camp environment. Two examples are Ernst Holzlohner, a German physiologist and university lecturer involved in this area of Nazi human experimentation, and Sigmund Rascher, an SS doctor. Both of these individuals were involved in sub-cooling experiments on behalf of the *Luftwaffe* at the Dachau concentration camp in 1942. These involved immersing selected prisoners in tanks of freezing cold water, who were then reheated using various methods. In one instance it was recorded that after one prisoner had been immersed in freezing cold water to simulate the worst possible winter conditions in the eastern territories he was removed and placed into boiling hot water, resulting in an agonising death. Rascher even went as far as to compile a table detailing the results of these experiments.

Other experiments involved the trial of cold-water immersion clothing for *Luftwaffe* aircrews. The prisoner would be forced into the suit before being placed into a tank of freezing water, simulating the winter temperatures of the North and Black seas, in some instances for hours at a time. Records reveal that immersion in water at a temperature of five degrees Centigrade is tolerable for a clothed male for up to 40–60 minutes, whereas raising the water temperature to fifteen degrees Centigrade increases tolerance to four to five hours. However, the ages of the subjects and their physical state when the experiment was conducted are not recorded. Cardiac arrhythmias are described in the Dachau Comprehensive Report as being slow, fast or irregular, without reference to any standard nomenclature. Ventricular fibrillation, known to be a common cause of death from hypothermia, and atrial fibrillation, the most frequent cardiac irregularity experienced with hypothermia, are given no consideration in the report. Instead, the doctors referred to 'atrial flutter', the only conventional designation mentioned, which is used to label a tracing of atrial fibrillation. The odd characterization of common clinical cardiac associated arrythmias

The Nazi Medical Experiments   37

suggests that those conducting these experiments had a lack of expertise in even the most basic clinical principles of cardiac physiology. An examination of Rascher's experimental records and statements provided by his colleagues suggested that it took between eighty minutes and six hours of cold-water immersion to kill naked victims, whereas victims wearing clothes expired after six to seven hours had elapsed. Either way the information regarding the lethality of these experiments is inconsistent and unreliable. It is highly likely, from transcripts provided by Rascher's assistants, that the mortality rates in freezing experiments were far higher than Rascher was happy to admit. For example, his assistants testified that in one series of seven such experiments some eighty to ninety of the prisoners died, whereas Rascher had stated that only thirteen died as a result. This alone is a vast area of study which could take up many more pages.

Other studies carried out involved placing prisoners outside naked in the open air for periods of up to several hours in temperatures as low as minus six degrees Centigrade. Exposing naked prisoners to the freezing winter conditions in Poland appeared to be a warped rite of passage in the death and labour camps of Nazi Germany. Twenty-year-old Polish girl Proksza Gertruda from Rynbik was arrested in 1942 for what was termed a 'political crime'. She was sentenced to two years imprisonment at the Auschwitz camp and arrived there on Monday 9 November 1942, where she was given the prisoner number 24137. In an interview conducted prior to her death in 1992, aged seventy-one, she recalled her arrival at the camp:

'It was freezing cold at that time of the year in Poland, yet they (the Nazi guards) shouted orders at us to remove all of our clothing. As we undressed the guards would stomp up and down the lines of prisoners shouting "schneller, schneller" (faster, faster) at us, we were hit with sticks and abused with filthy language. They (the guards) did not seem to be in a hurry to accommodate us or give us the striped uniform that prisoners had to wear in the camp.

38   The Nazi and Japanese Human Experimentation Programmes

They kept us standing out in the freezing cold for what must have been an hour or so, I don't remember. There were older people who became sick and fell down, if they didn't get up, they were dragged away and were not seen again. I remember the guards in their warm winter coats with their hands in their pockets walking up the lines as we stood trembling violently from the cold, they smiled at us and made typical sarcastic remarks like "it's cold today is it not"? They were bastards, but if you fell down you were dead, so you had to stand there and take it. When they moved us off to the block we were in just beyond the area where we had been forced to stand, we were prodded like cattle with sticks, shouted at and abused. Once inside the block we were issued these filthy uniforms, they had probably been removed from dead prisoners as they were not very clean and stank and were soiled with what looked like blood and faeces. It was never easy at that place and those of us sentenced to be freed afterwards did not get things any easier than the other prisoners in the camp. You always felt cold inside even in the summer months.'

Proksza was released after serving her full two years of incarceration at Auschwitz in November 1944. She returned to her former occupation working on the *Deutscher Reichsbahn* (German railway) issuing tickets to passengers. Her health had suffered due to her incarceration and the privations she endured, and this affected her up until her death in 1992. She was awarded the Auschwitz Survivors Cross on 9 May 1990.

High-altitude experiments

Another series of human experiments carried out at the Dachau concentration camp under the direction of Sigmund Rascher was intended to help German *Luftwaffe* pilots who had to eject from aircraft at high altitudes. The experiments were carried out to determine the chances of survival of German airmen exiting an aircraft at altitudes

The Nazi Medical Experiments   39

of 49–68,000 feet. In order for these experiments to be carried out a specially constructed low-pressure chamber was installed at the Dachau camp. The chamber was specifically designed to simulate conditions at altitudes of up to 68,000 feet (21,000 metres). In correspondence dated 5 April 1942, between Rascher and SS chief Heinrich Himmler, Rascher explains the results of a typical low-pressure experiment performed on a prisoner at Dachau, in which the prisoner was suffocated while Rascher and another unnamed doctor observed the victim's reaction. The victim was described by Rascher as being thirty-seven years of age and in good health before being murdered. Rascher described the victim's actions as he began to suffer from lack of oxygen, carefully timing the changes in behaviour. Rascher recalled how the victim began to wiggle his head some four minutes into the experiment; a minute later the victim appeared to be suffering from cramps before falling unconscious. Rascher then went on to explain how the victim lay unconscious, breathing only three times per minute, until he stopped breathing entirely thirty minutes after being deprived of oxygen. The victim then turned blue and began to foam at the mouth. An autopsy was carried out on the victim an hour later. In a letter of response to Rascher's letter dated 13 April 1942 Himmler insisted that Rascher continue with his high-altitude experiments, using prisoners condemned to death to 'determine whether these men could be recalled to life'. He then stated that if a victim could be successfully resuscitated, Himmler would order that 'the victim be pardoned to concentration camp for life'.

It was rumoured, and it seems probable, that Rascher performed vivisections on the brains of the victims who survived the initial high-altitude experiments. Of the 200 prisoners who were forced to take part in these high-altitude experiments, eighty died outright from the experience, while the rest were murdered.

40 The Nazi and Japanese Human Experimentation Programmes

Malaria experiments

From around February 1942 to April 1945 experiments were conducted at the Dachau concentration camp with the aim of developing immunisation drugs for the treatment of malaria. Doctors overseeing these experiments selected groups of those considered the healthiest prisoners, who were then placed in a controlled environment in which they were exposed to biting insects. Another method of inducing malaria was to inject the body of the prisoner with extracts of the mucous glands of female mosquitoes. Once the prisoner had contracted the disease they were then treated with various drugs to observe their effects on the condition. These experiments were seen as beneficial for the military operating in areas infested with mosquitoes, either in certain regions of Europe or the tropics. The prisoners were never told which drugs were being injected into their bodies during these experiments, and of the quoted figure of 1,200 prisoners who were used in these experiments more than half died as a result. Test subjects who survived the ordeal were left with permanent disabilities as a direct result of these tests.

Sulfonamide experiments

From July 1942 to around September 1943 experiments were conducted at the Ravensbruck concentration camp to investigate the effectiveness of sulfonamide, a synthetic antimicrobial agent, on a range of flesh wounds deliberately inflicted upon prisoners selected for the experiments. Sulfonamides are used to treat allergies and coughs, as well as having antifungal and antimalarial functions. In these experiments prisoners had wounds inflicted on their arms, legs or other areas of their body with knives, broken glass or other sharp implements. The wounds were then deliberately contaminated with powdered glass, splinters of wood, pieces of metal and soil. It is also rumoured that faecal material was introduced into the wounds of some subjects. Most of the wounds were infected with bacteria such as streptococcus, *Clostridium perfringens*

The Nazi Medical Experiments   41

(a major causative agent in gas gangrene) and *Clostridium tetani*, the causative agent in tetanus. The doctors would tie off blood vessels at either end of the wound to create conditions similar to battlefield wounds. In each case the wounds were left open to fester until they oozed thick yellow pus before sulfonamide was administered. The drug was usually given to the subject orally, but could also be injected into the subjects' veins. These procedures caused serious and potentially life-threatening conditions in many victims. Some had to undergo amputation of limbs when the sulfonamide and other drugs used did not have the desired effect. Those who had to undergo amputation were not given anaesthetic, and were then deemed unfit and either left to die in agony or murdered.

Julius Herbert, who was imprisoned at the Dachau camp, recalled seeing many prisoners over the course of two years who had undergone excruciatingly painful amputations of legs or arms following experiments, and they were simply dumped back into the prisoner barracks afterwards, where they were left to die. Julius recalled one young man who had had his left leg crudely sawn off before being tipped like an animal back through the barracks doors. The young man was in a very bad way and had lost a lot of blood. Julius described how the man's moaning and crying drove the other prisoners to euthanise him. He said it was 'one of the worst actions I have ever had to commit in my whole life, he was suffering with no hope of survival, you wouldn't let an animal suffer in that way so why a human being?' I asked Julius how he and the other prisoners euthanised the delirious victim and he replied 'we suffocated him, four of us did it, all four of us put our hands firmly over his mouth and nose and it was over mercifully quick. Had we not done that he may have lay there dying in agony for hours.'

Viral hepatitis experiments

From June 1943 until January 1945, at the Sachsenhausen and Natzweiler concentration camps, viral hepatitis experiments were

42 The Nazi and Japanese Human Experimentation Programmes

carried out on selected prisoners. SS chief Heinrich Himmler was well aware that these experiments would have a high mortality rate among the test subjects and suggested condemned criminals such as resistance group members should initially be used. Again, these tests were carried out for the benefit of the German armed forces. Test subjects would be restrained and injected with the virus, whereupon they would be subject to all manner of drug treatments so that the effect of each drug could be monitored. Viral hepatitis is a particularly unpleasant condition, the symptoms of which include fever, fatigue, loss of appetite, nausea, vomiting, abdominal pain, darkened urine, light coloured stools, joint pain and jaundice. On top of this the various drugs administered during the test phases of these experiments often had severe side effects of their own, such as severe headache, nausea, vomiting, stomach cramps, chronic insomnia, rectal bleeding, and loss of speech and/or vision. Unsurprisingly there were very few survivors of these abhorrent so-called experiments.

Electroshock experiments

The series of electroshock experiments conducted in the infamous Block 10 of the Auschwitz concentration camp are without doubt among some of the most depraved, disturbing and disgusting I have ever heard of to date. It appears from many reports that female subjects at the Auschwitz camp were often the target for these experiments. I recall from my own research work hearing a particular account from an eyewitness that was so sickening that I doubted at first that it could be true. Of course, later I heard similar things from other witnesses who had been at the Auschwitz camp, corroborating the fact that these incidents actually occurred. What is clear is that the electroshock therapy, now known as electroconvulsive therapy, conducted in Europe and particularly Third Reich Nazi Germany, is still a very neglected area of research, and few are aware of the facts. It may surprise some that the internationally recognised firm Siemens embraced this technology, regarding the practice as an honourable medical discipline. The Siemens company also assisted in the manufacture of electroshock therapy equipment used by the Nazis in their experiments on prisoners at Auschwitz. One such piece of equipment, manufactured by Siemens, was the Konvulsator. In Nazi Germany doctors had a free hand to practice electroshock therapy in the psychiatric hospitals, asylums and at the Auschwitz concentration camp. Electroshock therapies were nothing new to the world of medical science during the Nazi era and the practice had been in existence in professional and quack forms for many years. Traditionally electroshock therapies were used as a means of treating mental illness in lunatic asylums. The therapy applied to mental patients in the asylum system did, however, differ greatly from the torture inflicted under the Nazi regime. The Nazis used electroshock therapy more as a means of killing or torturing subjects rather than curing them of any psychological ills. It is true that mild electroshock therapy had been observed to improve the mental conditions of some subjects suffering from mental illnesses such as schizophrenia. Electroshock therapy apparatus was installed at Auschwitz III in Poland and the working camp of the IG Farben-Werk in Monowitz in 1944. With the unofficial agreement of the SS camp physicians Eduard Wirths and Horst Fischer, the Polish detainee physician Zenon Drohocki, assisted by a Dutch engineer detainee, wanted to treat sick detainees with the apparatus in the neuropsychiatric department which he had established inside the Monowitz camp detainee hospital. Drohocki was somewhat instrumental in increasing Nazi interest in electroshock therapy, perhaps as a means of saving his own skin after attempting to flee to Switzerland to escape the Nazis, very conveniently carrying design papers for an electroshock therapy apparatus in his rucksack. It appears that having been caught by the authorities Drohocki then used these technical papers as a bargaining chip. The forms of electroshock therapy carried out on prisoners at Auschwitz could not be construed as therapeutic. A selected prisoner would be brought into the treatment room and strapped down to a table or chair and electrodes would be

44 The Nazi and Japanese Human Experimentation Programmes

placed on the head, chest and other areas of the body and electrical currents of varying intensity would then be passed through their bodies. As there was no diagnosis of mental illness in some of these prisoners one can only assume that these procedures were carried out with no particular medical or scientific objective, and that these subjects were merely being subjected to torture, after which they were murdered. Perhaps one of the most chilling accounts conveyed to me came during an interview with an elderly German woman named Madalina Schildt, which took place some years ago. Madalina was a seventeen-year-old who received specific orders to report to the Ravensbruck camp located in the Furstenburg area of Havel in Germany in July 1943. Her role at the Ravensbruck camp was little more than a lowly junior office worker. Madalina recalled:

'I also reported to other areas around the facility including the medical block there delivering various documents to the different offices and departments. It was through the course of my duties going to the medical block that I witnessed twice some form of sexually orientated electrical medical experiments being conducted on two young Jewish women, both of whom subsequently died after the procedures. I remember seeing the one Jewish woman who was comatose and strapped down to a medical examination table. Her legs had been raised and held apart in an apparatus resembling a gynaecological chair. At first sight I thought the woman must have been in childbirth, or the doctors present were attempting to induce labour or something, I didn't know but I was curious and looked closer. It was then I could see that there was some kind of plug inserted fully into her vagina orifice. The plug had several electrical wires attached to it which in turn were connected to some sort of panel with dials, switches and gauges on it. Before I could witness anything more, I was told to leave as I was only there to hand over some paperwork to one of the physicians in charge of the block. It was two days later in the same

The Nazi Medical Experiments   45

room of the same block that I witnessed another young Jewish female prisoner restrained in exactly the same manner as the last one I saw. She was restrained with her legs raised and held apart with electrical wiring attached to her vagina. This time there was not only some kind of plug with wiring attached inside her vagina but wires with these what looked like small jaws or clamps at their ends, and these were attached to the clitoral region. On this occasion the experiment was already underway when I entered the room. One of the doctors present was turning a dial on the same control panel, moving them clockwise and counter-clockwise. As the doctor moved these dials the woman's body convulsed and her back appeared to arch upwards violently. I noticed the skin around her wrists where the leather straps held her down was turning white and every time the doctor turned the dial on the panel her body convulsed, arched and she moaned out loudly. Another doctor snapped at me "what do you want, what is your duty here"? I handed over several documents contained in a brown envelope before being told to leave again. I had no idea what they were doing and could not have asked any questions about it. I thought about it a lot afterwards and imagined had it been me what that would have been like. From my own assumptions there was little in the way of medical science to be learned from such a procedure and that it was some form of sexual torture or sexual manipulation, but for what purpose? All that I know is that after both experiments had finished two dead bodies left that room and were quickly disposed of.'

A colleague of Madalina's witnessed a similar experiment while at the Ravensbruck camp and confided in her after the war what he had seen. Madalina continued:

'My colleague was one of the administration staff in the medical block at the camp. He saw a Jewish male prisoner taken into the room where the electrical apparatus was installed. He told me they put electrodes on the Jew's testicles and even inserted an electrode into the man's anus before administering an electrical current. He said that the prisoner cried out in agony, struggled in the restraints for some seconds before falling into unconsciousness. They brought him round by pouring cold water over his head before continuing with the experiment. The man again struggled violently and there was some involuntary urinating before the man again lost consciousness. The man was then removed from the restraints and taken away. Whether he was alive or dead he could not say as he did not see what happened to the man after that. My colleague told me that electrodes were placed all over the bodies of prisoners during the experiments, on their breasts and nipples, ears, noses, genitals and legs and also inserted into the anus, ears, vagina and penis of both the male and female prisoners.'

It must be pointed out here that Madalina Schildt was no willing volunteer or participant and had been forced to report to the Ravensbruck camp after several heated altercations with the local BDM (*Bund Deutscher Madel* – the female branch of the Hitler Youth). She was ordered to report for Reich service work at Ravensbruck as a punishment for refusing orders and what the local Nazi BDM authority termed 'poor conduct', and she was there until the winter of 1944.In many ways she was very fortunate to not have been sent to one of the concentration camps herself.

Phosphorous burn experiments

The chemical phosphorous of the type formulated for military application is arguably one of the most lethal and feared weaponised chemical elements adapted for use in warfare. The lethality of phosphorous cannot be reiterated enough. During the First World War the chemical white phosphorous was used in both illumination

The Nazi Medical Experiments   47

and incendiary projectiles fired by artillery on the battlefield. It was also used in mortar weapons of various calibres. White phosphorous comes in the form of a translucent waxy solid that quickly becomes yellow when exposed to light. When enclosed within the metal body of a carrier munition the chemical is perfectly safe to handle. Yet when the chemical is exposed to oxygen, such as when the carrier munition bursts, the white phosphorous self-ignites the moment it is exposed to oxygen. It burns at a over 800 degrees Celsius. In the First World War white phosphorous used in artillery shells and mortars caused horrific burn injuries. There were incidences in which victims of white phosphorus shell attacks spontaneously combusted in their hospital beds due to small traces of the chemical remaining in their wounds. For example, if you took a pellet of white phosphorous the size of a match head and dropped it into the palm of your hand it would burn right through to the other side. If immersed in water, it becomes inactive, yet the moment it is taken out of the water and makes contact with oxygen it will reignite and burn furiously. Nazi doctors conducted experiments on behalf of the German army on concentration camp prisoners by deliberately exposing them to white phosphorous so as to devise methods of treating the subsequent burns, which were frequently encountered on the battlefield. Concentration camp victims were usually restrained in chairs or on surgical tables before pellets or larger pieces of the white phosphorous material were dropped on to various areas of their bodies. White phosphorus burns very deeply into human tissue to the extent that it can burn through vital organs, veins and blood vessels, causing death or permanent damage and/or disability. It was noted that at the Buchenwald concentration camp phosphorous material was extracted from incendiary bomb tubes and placed on the bodies of prisoners. Following the experiment, the victim would be treated with a cocktail of pharmaceutical preparations to ascertain which best alleviated the problems associated with the phosphorus burns. The Buchenwald phosphorous trials were conducted between 1943 and 1944.

48   The Nazi and Japanese Human Experimentation Programmes

Experiments with poison and toxins

Between December 1943 and October 1944, experiments took place at the Buchenwald concentration camp to observe the effect of various poisons on prisoners at the camp. The poisons were often administered secretly and placed in the unsuspecting prisoner's food. The victims either died as a result of the poison or were murdered immediately after consumption in order for autopsies to study the effects. In September 1944, records reveal that prisoners were shot with bullets containing a poisonous substance, and were then tortured until death occurred. Some male Jewish prisoners also had poisonous substances scrubbed or injected into their skin, often causing boils filled with black fluid to form on the body. The kinds of poisons administered to the prisoners ranged from naturally occurring substances such as cyanide, arsenic, strychnine, carbolic acid and xylyl bromide, to synthetic toxins such as tabun. It is recorded that tabun can be destroyed with bleaching powder (calcium hypochlorite), though the reaction of the two compounds mixing will in turn produce the poisonous gas cyanogen chloride.

Experiments on twins

The medical experiments carried out on twins, particularly those at the Auschwitz camp, are among the most infamous of the Nazi genetic/medical crimes. The experiments conducted on sets of twins at Auschwitz were carried out under the direction of SS physician *Hauptsturmfuhrer* (captain) Josef Mengele. Mengele was the most prominent of a group of Nazi doctors responsible for carrying out experiments which in almost all cases caused grievous injury, suffering and death to prisoner victims, including many children. Mengele used the Nazi racial theories of race and eugenics to justify a broad spectrum of medical experiments on Jews and Roma gypsies. Many of the subjects selected by Mengele for his experiments died as a direct result of the procedures carried out on them, or were murdered in order to

The Nazi Medical Experiments   49

facilitate post-mortem examinations. It is one of the most galling facts of all that Mengele was able to escape justice for his crimes, fleeing to South America as the Third Reich collapsed. He was sly enough to insist that he did not receive the tattooed SS blood group number on his underarm. This was a feature that ensured that all captured SS personnel could be identified. Although Mengele did fall into the hands of the Allied forces, his lack of the tattoo meant that he was not detained for further investigation and slunk away to freedom before his true identity could be ascertained.

Josef Rudolf Mengele was born into a Catholic family on 16 March 1911 in Gunzburg, in the Kingdom of Bavaria, German Empire. He was the eldest of three sons of Walburga and Karl Mengele. Mengele's father was the founder of the Karl Mengele & Sons company, which was later renamed Mengele Agrartechnik, a company which built agricultural machinery. Josef was described as a highly academic pupil at school, developing an interest in music, art, and skiing. Upon completion of his high school education, he went on to study philosophy in Munich, which was also the beating heart of the Nazi Party movement. Mengele attended the University of Bonn, and it was there that he took his first preliminary medical examination. In 1931 he began his association with the Nazi Party, joining the paramilitary organization that was soon absorbed into the SA (*Sturmabteilung* or storm troopers). In 1935 Mengele gained a PhD in anthropology from the University of Munich and in January 1937 he joined the Institute for Hereditary Biology and Racial Hygiene in Frankfurt, where he worked under Otmar Freiherr von Verschuer, a German geneticist with a particular interest in the medical and genetic features of twins. During this period Mengele himself developed the same obsessive interest in twins and, as von Verschuer's colleague, Mengele focussed on the genetic factors that result in a cleft lip and palate, or a cleft chin. His thesis on this subject earned him a *cum laude* doctorate in medicine (MD) from the University of Frankfurt in 1938. It should be noted that both of these degrees were revoked by the issuing universities in the 1960s as

50 The Nazi and Japanese Human Experimentation Programmes

information became available about the crimes committed by Mengele during his time at Auschwitz, where he earned the nickname 'The Angel of Death'.

Mengele's mentor von Verschuer wrote a letter of recommendation praising Mengele's attributes, combined with a natural ability to verbally present complex explanations in understandable terms. Much of the work that Mengele would go on to publish was viewed as in keeping with the views of the scientific mainstream of the day and would have likely been accepted as valid scientific endeavour even outside Nazi Germany. Mengele saw active service with the German military during the Second World War. As a member of the 5th SS Panzer (Tank) Division *Wiking* Mengele was a battalion medical officer. In the course of his duties in the Ukraine he rescued two German tank crew from their burning tank and was subsequently awarded the Iron Cross 1st Class, the Wound Badge in Black, and the Medal for the Care of the German People. Mengele was declared unfit for further active service in mid-1942 when he was seriously injured in action near Rostov-on-Don. After recuperating from his injuries, he was transferred to the headquarters of the SS Race and Settlement Main Office in Berlin. It was around this time that Mengele resumed his association with von Verschuer, who had since risen through the ranks and was now director of the Kaiser Wilhelm Institute of Anthropology, Human Heredity, and Eugenics.

It was through a recommendation from von Verschuer that Mengele applied for a transfer to the concentration camp service. His application was accepted, and he was posted to Auschwitz, where he was appointed by SS-*Standortarzt* Eduard Wirths (who as previously noted was senior medical officer at the Auschwitz camp) to the position of head physician of the *Zigeunerfamilienlager* (the Romani family camp at Birkenau, a sub-camp located within the main Auschwitz complex). It was here that Mengele made his weekly visits to the hospital barracks and gave personal orders that any prisoners who had failed to recover after a period of two weeks should be sent to the gas chambers.

The Nazi Medical Experiments   51

Mengele was also placed in charge of prisoner selections as they arrived at the camp. This was a task he relished and carried out even when not directly assigned to do so, in the hope of finding fresh subjects for his experiments, most notably on twins. Most of the other SS doctors loathed the stressful and unpleasant elements of the selection process, but Mengele enjoyed this duty, going about it with an air of flamboyance and often smiling and whistling. Mengele was also one of the SS doctors responsible for supervising the administration of Zyklon B, the cyanide-based pesticide that was used to kill prisoners in the gas chambers. Mengele was active in this role in crematoria IV and V and again it was noted that he went about this work in a jovial, happy manner, never once expressing disgust at the disturbing scenes he would have undoubtedly witnessed.

In 1943 the Romani camp experienced an outbreak of Noma – a gangrenous bacterial infection of the mouth and face. Mengele immediately initiated a study programme to determine the origins of the disease and to develop an antidote. He then enlisted the services of Jewish paediatrician (and former professor at the University of Prague) Berthold Epstein, who was imprisoned at the camp, to assist him in finding measures to treat the disease in the Romani prisoners. Mengele ascertained that the prisoners should be isolated in separate barracks, where several of the Romani children were murdered and had their heads removed. The heads were placed in preservative fluids along with other internal organs removed during dissection and these were sent to the SS Medical Academy in Graz and other institutions for study purposes. This particular area of research was still being conducted up to the point when the Romani camp was liquidated, and the remaining prisoners murdered, in 1944.

The Auschwitz camp also enabled Mengele to continue with his research into anthropological studies and heredity. As he had thousands of prisoners within the camp at his disposal, no consideration was given to their health, safety or physical and mental wellbeing, or the suffering they endured as a result of his experiments.

52   The Nazi and Japanese Human Experimentation Programmes

Mengele's medical interests focused primarily on identical twins, prisoners with heterochromia iridum (eyes of two different colours), dwarfs and those prisoners with physical abnormalities. Funding for Mengele's work was provided by the German Research Foundation (*Deutsche Forschungsgemeinschaft*) at the request of von Verschuer, who in turn received reports and consignments of specimens from Mengele. The grant funding approved for Mengele's work enabled the construction of a purpose-built pathology lab, which was attached to crematorium II at Auschwitz II-Birkenau. In some respects Mengele's prisoners did fare slightly better than the other prisoners at Auschwitz: they were fed food of better quality, and their barracks were generally more comfortable than the standard ones used by the other prisoners. Being one of Mengele's prisoners also gave one a temporary stay of execution, and so long as a prisoner had some value, he or she was kept alive.

The inherent contradiction in Mengele's personality came to the fore when dealing with his child subjects in the camp. When he visited the children he intended to use in his experiments he would introduce himself as 'Uncle Mengele'. He would bring bags of sweets with him to share out among the children, and he expressed warmth and friendship toward them with his smile and kind gestures. However, Mengele was a man with a total lack of empathy, who was anti-Semitic in the extreme. He was convinced that the Jews should be eliminated as an inferior and dangerous race. He also murdered an unspecified number of prisoners through lethal injection, shooting, beating, and of course, the experiments he conducted, which often proved fatal. A former prisoner doctor at the Auschwitz camp recalled of Mengele:

'He was capable of being so kind to the children, to have them become fond of him, to bring them sweets, to think of small details in their daily lives, and to do things we would genuinely admire, and then, next to that, the crematoria, smoke and these children tomorrow or even in half an hour, he is going to send them there. Well, this is where the anomaly lay.'

The Nazi Medical Experiments   53

It is not possible to catalogue every single medical and scientific abuse that Mengel was responsible for, but a few examples of the many include twins being subject to the unnecessary amputation of limbs, intentionally infecting one twin with the typhus bacteria or some other disease and transfusing the blood of one twin into the other. Those twins who survived these procedures were then murdered and subject to dissection. Their heads were often removed by surgical scalpel and their eyes, brains and tongues were sometimes removed from for preservation and study. If one twin died during a particular procedure the other twin would be quickly killed in order to allow a comparative post-mortem for research purposes. Mengele's eye experiments sought to change the eye colour of some of his subjects by injecting chemicals directly into their eyes while they were fully conscious. The subject would be restrained on an operating table with eye clamps in place to prevent the victim from blinking or attempting to close his or her eyes during the procedure, which would have been excruciatingly painful. Subjects with heterochromatic eyes were often killed so their eyes could be removed from their heads and sent to various institutions for study and further dissection. Most of the institutions receiving these body parts had affiliations with the SS.

Experiments carried out on dwarfs involved taking measurements, drawing blood, the unnecessary extraction of healthy teeth, and treatments with various drugs and X-rays. Most of Mengele's test subjects were kept alive for a period of around two weeks before being sent to the gas chambers. It was noted that after the subjects had been gassed their bodies were immersed in sulphuric acid baths so their skeletal remains could be sent to Berlin for further medical and scientific study. Pregnant women also fell victim to Mengele's barbarous activities. In an unpublished manuscript on the Mengele atrocities, written by a Mr Alex Mueller, whose mother had been imprisoned at Auschwitz and had dictated her experiences, she alleged that she had seen Mengele open up the belly of a pregnant Jewish female with a surgical knife and remove the unborn baby from her womb. The female

54   The Nazi and Japanese Human Experimentation Programmes

in question was some three weeks away from giving birth when this procedure was carried out. She died shortly after the procedure along with her infant, which had been placed in one of the sinks and left to die. Auschwitz survivor Alex Dekel was able to confirm that Mengele did carry out vivisections on prisoners without anaesthetic. Alex reported that during these vivisections internal organs such as kidneys, livers, hearts and stomachs were removed. Another Auschwitz survivor recalled how Mengele had removed his kidney without anaesthesia and he was forced to return to work without any aftercare or painkilling medication. Another recollection by an eyewitness named Vera Alexander reveals that Mengele sewed two Romani twins together back-to-back, in some crude attempt at creating conjoined twins. It was reported that the twins developed gangrene along the stitched areas, where thick yellow pus was seen to leak from the stitching. These unfortunate twins were said to have been euthanised by their own parents to end their suffering.

It may also have been Mengele or one of his assistants who was responsible for the murder of fourteen-year-old Polish girl Czeslawa Kwoka. A photograph of Czeslawa taken at Auschwitz, her face swollen and bruised from a beating she had received just minutes before the photo was taken, in many ways represents the horror of Nazism in its entirety. Czeslawa was born on 15 August 1928 in Wolka Ziojecka, a small village near the city of Zamosc in south-eastern Poland. Sadly, very little is known about Czeslawa's life prior to the Nazi invasion of Poland in 1939. Czeslawa's mother's name was Katarznya and the family were little more than poor farmers. Life for Czeslawa and her family was destroyed in the summer of 1942 when the Nazis took steps to Germanize the territories around Zamosc. With the implementation of this plan Polish families living in the area were subject to forced expulsion from their homes; their properties were taken over by German settlers brought in from other areas of Europe such as Bosnia, Romania and Luxembourg. The Nazi resettlement process began on 27 November 1942 and Wolka Zlojecka was among the first Polish communities to be affected by the Nazi plan. Czeslawa

The Nazi Medical Experiments   55

and all of the other Polish nationals in residence in the village, except for those who had been fortunate enough to escape before the Nazis came, were rounded up and arrested. Czeslawa and her family were sent to a transit camp at Zamosc where they were held until their destination was decided. Czeslawa was one of approximately 30,000 children from the Zamosc region who was rounded up for deportation. The younger children, including babies, and the elderly were separated from their families before being sent to what the Nazi authorities called 'rest villages', which were dispersed around Poland. In these so called 'rest villages' they were basically left to fend for themselves. Czeslawa, aged fourteen, was considered old enough to be sent for forced labour. Most of those selected for forced labour tasks ended up being sent to work in Germany, but Czeslawa and her mother were instead sent to the Auschwitz concentration camp on 13 December 1942. Each new prisoner was photographed on arrival. When it came to Czeslawa's turn the photographer, who was a Polish political prisoner named Wilhelm Brasse, recalled:

'Before Czeslawa came in to have her photograph taken, she was confused and frightened and did not understand what orders one of the female Kapos were shouting at her.'

The Kapo in question, who remains unknown, was a privileged prisoner given the task of supervising other prisoners in the camp. These Kapos were seen as the lowest of the low and traitors to their fellow countrymen. Brasse continued:

'the Kapo had beaten Czeslawa up hitting her hard about the head and face quite severely and I noticed she looked as if she had been crying, her face was swollen, and her lip cut and bleeding.'

It is not known what forced labour duties Czeslawa was put to work on during her brief life at Auschwitz, but it is known that her mother

56   The Nazi and Japanese Human Experimentation Programmes

Katarzyna died at Auschwitz on 18 February 1943, some two months after arriving. Czeslawa died less than one month later on 12 March, yet the cause of her death is still subject to some conjecture. Most reliable sources, based on the general evidence, agree that Czeslawa was murdered by having an injection of carbolic acid administered directly into her heart. This would almost certainly have been carried out either by Mengele himself or one of his colleagues. The photo of fourteen-year-old Czeslawa Kwoka is one of the most haunting and saddest of the Holocaust images I have seen during my research. It never fails to move me and is a reminder of the sheer evil and perverted violence that the Nazi era espoused, which should never be forgotten or censored from modern history.

Mengele fled to South America after the collapse of the German military and the Third Reich. For a while he lived the high life in Argentina, which at the time was under the rule of Juan Domingo Peron, which shared many of the political and social characteristics of fascism. The country had declared itself neutral until 27 March 1945 when it finally made a declaration of war against the Axis powers. Mengele was not alone in fleeing to Argentina. Many high- and low-ranking Nazis were able to flee to the country along with their extended families, often using stolen gold as a means of buying their freedom. However, things changed for Mengele after the capture of Adolf Eichmann, who had also fled to Argentina and had lived there for some time under an alias. Eichmann was kidnapped in a spectacular operation mounted by agents of the Israeli Mossad organisation, who then transported Eichmann to Israel to stand trial for his war crimes. Eichmann was found guilty and was hanged on 1 June 1962 at Ayalon Prison, Ramla, Israel. Mossad, as the Israeli national intelligence agency, were also on Mengele's trail and almost succeeded in capturing him at one point. Mengele fled and went to ground, living the rest of his life in constant fear, just as his victims had done. Many say that this was a fitting punishment for one of the most evil and sadistic doctors of the

The Nazi Medical Experiments   57

Third Reich. Mengele died by drowning after suffering a stroke while swimming off the coast of Bertioga when he was sixty-seven years old.

A name seldom heard of in connection with Nazi medical experimentation is that of doctor Herta Oberheuser. She was born on 15 May 1911 in Cologne, German Empire. While little information is available on her childhood, my research has thrown up some details of the early life of this woman who would become one of the most sadistic of the few female doctors in Nazi Germany. Oberheuser's parents were committed Nazis, fully embracing the National Socialist cause. At school Herta was described as a bright, intuitive and highly intelligent girl. She was not unattractive as a young girl, yet those who associated with her recalled as she grew older recall that her face took on a cold, cruel appearance and she possessed a fierce temper. Kyla Pacchianoa, the daughter of Italian immigrants who lived in Cologne, recalled:

'She was quite ordinary in most respects, and she had her group of friends whom she liked and who liked her. She was known for having a vicious temper though. I recall her getting into a fight with another girl once at school. It started off as most fights do with name calling and silly things like that. I could see that Herta was becoming very irritated, when she stared at someone in anger her eyes were very scary, they resembled those of an angry dog about to attack. In the end the name calling turned into a physical fight, Herta fought like a devil throwing vicious punches and she soon won the fight, the other girl having received a bloodied nose gave up and hastily beat her retreat. The girl in question and her group of friends never bothered Herta again.'

Herta became a member of the female Hitler Youth, the *Bund Deutscher Madel* (BDM), before it became compulsory for all young people to join. She excelled in the ranks of the BDM and possessed good leadership skills and athletic ability and earned the admiration of many of the other girls and the BDM leaders. Herta studied and earned her medical degree

58   The Nazi and Japanese Human Experimentation Programmes

in Bonn in 1937, specialising in dermatology. Afterwards she enrolled in the Nazi Party as a medical intern, although she did not have a full licence allowing her to practice medicine in an unsupervised capacity. Herta's records confirmed that she became a doctor within the BDM, and it was stated that her abilities as a physician were highly respected and trusted. In the BDM Herta treated the various minor wounds and skin abrasions often encountered while partaking in the various sports, marching and hiking and camping activities. But how did this quiet – yet sometimes fiery – young woman become so infamous for medical cruelty, leading some to nickname her 'the devil's daughter'?

This is relatively easy to explain. In 1940 Oberheuser was appointed to serve as an assistant to Doctor Karl Gebhardt, who was then chief surgeon of the SS and also SS chief Heinrich Himmler's personal physician. In 1942 Oberheuser and Gebhardt arrived at the Ravensbruck concentration camp. Their medical objectives at the camp were to investigate various methods of treating wound infections. Far from actually treating the wounds and skin infections of prisoners at the camp, the pair deliberately infected the wounds of prisoners to observe the rate and depth of infection, especially when foreign bodies were introduced into the wounds. The pair would place glass splinters, fragments of wood, rusty nails, sawdust and even dog faeces into wounds, sometimes closing the wound with a suture to observe how the wound festered and the physical effects upon the prisoner. They would sometimes make incisions in limbs in order to expose areas of bone. The wound would then be left uncovered to be contaminated by the flies which infested the filthy conditions of the camp. It was also alleged that insects were collected from within and around the prisoner latrines. These insects had been crawling over unimaginable filth, and were then placed on the prisoners' open wounds and covered with a fine mesh to prevent them from escaping.

Oberheuser also made incisions in the leg of one female prisoner then placed a plaster cast over the wound. The plaster cast was only removed when the smell from the wound became unbearable, with

The Nazi Medical Experiments   59

pus oozing from out of the cast. When her victims cried out for water Oberheuser obliged only after filling the cup half with vinegar. She also removed moles and warts from the skin of prisoners with a scalpel and without any anaesthetic. In fact, both Oberheuser and Gebhardt rarely gave their subjects anaesthetic or pain relief during their experiments. Oberheuser also experimented on children, injecting their bodies with Evipan, which was an anaesthetic drug. Once the drug had begun to take effect Oberheuser would then perform vivisection on the child, who would be fully aware of what was happening yet helpless to stop her and unable to feel anything. During these vile procedures organs would be removed and amputations of limbs carried out. Many of her child victims would be dead within three to five minutes of the Evipan being injected, but some died of shock as a result of being able to witness what was being done to them.

The experiments carried out by Oberheuser and Gebhardt caused the deaths of many prisoners at the Ravensbruck camp and, like those already discussed, did not contribute to medical understanding as the outcomes were entirely predictable: infection, fever, blood poisoning and death. Oberheuser in particular appeared to enjoy watching the suffering of the prisoners she conducted experiments on. At the Nuremberg Doctors' Trial Oberheuser was the only female defendant. She escaped the hangman's noose and on 20 August 1947 was sentenced to serve twenty years in prison. However, her luck continued and despite being found guilty of the criminal acts described above, her sentence was reduced to just five years as time already spent in custody was taken into account. Oberheuser was released from prison in 1952 and attempted to resume her career. As soon as the authorities discovered that she was working as a doctor her medical licence was revoked by the court of Schleswig-Holstein. Unable to practice medicine, Oberheuser faded into obscurity, and little was heard of her again until her death in 1978 in a nursing home in Germany. Karl Gebhardt was hanged for war crimes and crimes against humanity on 2 June 1948 at Landsberg Prison in Bavaria. Many of the surviving victims of Herta Oberheuser suffered

60   The Nazi and Japanese Human Experimentation Programmes

lifelong pain and disability due to the procedures she carried out on their bodies. Most were left in shock that she could get away with the murder of so many men, women and children. One of Oberheuser's victims said to me in an interview:

'Can you imagine yourself losing consciousness, with that cruel soulless face and piercing evil eyes being what might be the last thing you saw? All the operations I had to correct the damage that she had done to my body, all the pain I had to endure unnecessarily and would continue to suffer probably all of my life, all of the quality of a healthy life I should have had was taken away by her. I lived, yes, I am thankful for that and to be able to tell my story to you. Had I had the chance would I have killed her for what she did to me? Yes, I probably would have at one time but the way I look at it now is if those who fail to face justice for their crimes in this world then they will face their retribution in the next one, I believe in that.'

Chapter 5

Aktion T4 – the Nazi Euthanasia Programme

The Aktion T4 programme – the Nazi euthanasia programme – affected German society as a whole, not just those of Jewish, Romani, Polish or eastern descent. It is separate from the general medical experiments performed by Nazi doctors on concentration camp inmates and requires distinct analysis.

The Aktion T4 programme was a specific medical intervention designed to kill individuals with psychological and physically debilitating disorders. The programme soon expanded to include other individuals, such as the elderly, who were considered a burden on national resources and finances, not only for the Nazi medical profession as a whole but also wider Nazi society. If any naivety existed about the fratricidal reality of Hitler's Third Reich, then the implementation of Aktion T4 should have made the moral, social and political climate perfectly clear, even by 1939 standards. The term 'euthanasia' is somewhat questionable, as it was merely a euphemistic or non-direct term for what some describe as 'clandestine murder'. However, Aktion T4 was certainly not a clandestine operation. This was cold-blooded murder, carried out in the plain sight of the society in which it was taking place. Nazi society was fully aware of the existence of Aktion T4; some even celebrated it and a great many more lived in fear of it.

The mentally ill and insane were often murdered behind the closed doors of the asylum system, but those with less severe mental impairments, or physical disability, who were otherwise perfectly able to operate within society, were also ruthlessly targeted. German young

62   The Nazi and Japanese Human Experimentation Programmes

people were educated to accept the racial and physiological doctrines taught to them as upholders of the new Nazi Aryan race. Thus the severity of the methods employed by the Nazi leadership was never open to question or debate in the normal sense. The Hitler Youth generation were educated to understand that they could not be remorseful about the removal of inferior biological and physiological traits possessed by certain groups of individuals within Nazi society. There were of course many who spoke out against such barbaric social practices as Aktion T4, but these individuals were quickly silenced, usually under the threat of arrest, execution or being sent to one of the concentration camps. The Roman Catholic Church, which had not taken a stand on the 'Jewish question', protested about the so-called 'mercy killings'. Count Clemens August von Galen, the bishop of Munster, openly criticised the Aktion T4 programme, arguing that it was the duty of Christians to oppose the taking of human life, even if this stance cost them their own lives.

Adolf Hitler issued a directive to his personal physician, doctor Karl Brandt, and chief of the Chancellery of the Führer, Philipp Bouhler, which set the wheels of the Aktion T4 euthanasia programme in motion. Hitler had backdated his order to 1 September 1939 in an attempt to make Aktion T4 seem like a wartime measure born out of pure necessity. With the implementation of Hitler's plan, a whole bureaucracy of physicians were required to evaluate and decide who should be put to death under what were termed 'mercy killings', or the deaths of those who had a 'life unworthy of living'. Far from being racially or biologically motivated, the most important factor in an individual being selected as either fit or unfit was financial. If an individual was unable to work, for example, the Nazis would refer to them as 'burdensome lives' or 'useless eaters'. All psychiatric institutions, hospitals and homes for the chronically ill within the Reich territory were surveyed. Medical experts reviewed forms sent by institutions throughout Germany, but did not examine patients or read their medical records. They were given the power to play God and decide

Aktion T4 – the Nazi Euthanasia Programme   63

who lived and who died based on economic criteria. Many selected for elimination had a simple 'X' drawn through their medical records.

The methods employed by the Aktion T4 programme began with starvation, but this was by no means a quick way of killing someone or giving them the prescribed 'good death'. More efficient ways of killing were soon devised, and these involved teams of doctors injecting lethal poisons directly into the hearts of their victims. Once dead the corpses were often removed and incinerated, leaving no trace. Lethal injection, although found to be very effective, was still time consuming and it took teams of ten to twenty doctors many weeks or months to eradicate selected patients from whole asylums, hospitals and homes for the chronically ill. Programme administrators addressed this issue by establishing six gas chambers in Germany and Austria, primarily for the use by Aktion T4. Like some of the gas chambers in the concentration camps the gas chambers were disguised as showers. Victims were taken from either their families or places of care, and the SS staff in charge of arranging transport to the gas chambers wore white coats to maintain the charade that the process was a medical procedure. Once the victims had reached their destination and had been killed falsified death certificates were issued and signed by physicians, along with condolence letters and ashes of the victims contained in urns. An example of the above was described to me many years ago when I was researching material for what would become my first book, *Hitler's Girls – Doves Amongst Eagles* (Pen & Sword, 2017).

The Hitler Youth far from being just a Nazi political organisation for Germanys young people served the far more sinister role of weeding out the weaklings or those considered mentally inept by the Nazi authorities. There have been countless stories of how once the Nazis had come to power that the children of Germany came under the close scrutiny of the state in terms of their racial cleanliness, physical capabilities and even their general physical characteristics. For example, Elise Bettmann a schoolgirl in Nazi occupied Austria recalled how all the girls and boys in her school were suddenly the subject of intense

64   The Nazi and Japanese Human Experimentation Programmes

and often intrusive medical examinations around the time when the Aktion T4 programme began to accelerate. She recalled the following incidents within her school:

'There was a girl in our class who I knew but I could not say that she and I were ever close friends. We would say hello if we passed each other and sometimes we would play in the same group in the playground. She had this strange deformity of her mouth it was sort of crooked and yes it did make her look odd. When the medical examinations began this deformity as they referred to it did not go unnoticed by the doctors who came to the school on a number of occasions. The one day she did not return to the school and no reasons were given for her absence. Other children disappeared too as there were one or two with what I would say in the view of the Nazi state were mental impairments. These children were not mentally retarded in any way they were just slower learners than the rest of us, but the doctors considered anyone who could not read and write correctly or conduct physical exercises in the way the other children could as being imbeciles. The best specimens were separated from what were considered the poor mental and physical ones and these poor souls were sent away to clinics. This all seems a bit hypocritical when one considers that propaganda minister Goebbels was born with deformities and walked with a limp due to a club foot. The parents of these children had no rights to question the regime as to their decisions and they could not even visit their children while they were held in these so-called clinics. I was told that these children would have undergone various tests and once those tests had been exhausted the children were often given a lethal injection to euthanize them. Causes of death were falsified on medical documents and these were then sent to the families who were told they could collect their child's ashes. There was no evidence of the murder and many families by this time were too frightened to kick up a fuss. I know there were some that did attempt to confront the authorities and they were quickly silenced through various means. The threat of being sent to one of the camps, imprisonment or even

Aktion T4 – the Nazi Euthanasia Programme   65

treason was enough to buy their silence in many cases. It was and still is a dreadful scar on our history. Of course, we didn't find these things out until some years after the war had ended. Many of these children including the ones from the school I attended were euthanized under the Aktion T4 programme. No trace of them was left and from what I understand their only remains were as names on a typed document list and I believe some of these lists of men, women and children murdered under the Aktion T4 programme were used as evidence in the Allied war crimes tribunal.'

The mass murder programme of Aktion T4 in 1939 was a precursor to the Holocaust which we recognise today. The killing centres that many of the handicapped were transported to were in effect antecedents of Nazi extermination camps. Those physicians who became experts in the technology of cold-blooded murder in the late 1930s later staffed the medical blocks of the extermination camps. These, we now understand, were men who had abandoned any sense of moral, professional, and ethical inhibition. It is believed that around 200,000 people died as a result of the Aktion T4 programme.

Chapter 6

Elsa's Return

In 1944 Elsa Lanneberger (see Chapter 2) was thirty years old. She had left her home in Germany at the age of eighteen to stay with relatives in the USA in order to be able to continue studying to become a physician. Now fully qualified, she volunteered to join the mobile surgical/hospital units in Europe in the wake of the Allied invasion of Normandy in 1944. Elsa recalled:

'I had studied in America and with war breaking out in Europe in 1939 my family begged me to stay where I was until it was all over. This was not easy at first, I was able to complete my studies and I began working at a hospital in Illinois. Of course, I was questioned a lot at first as I had the distinctive German accent and some people made nasty remarks to me. I was even questioned by a department of the US military authority on one occasion. I think they were curious of me more than anything and once they had learned my story, they left me alone. My family also received visits from the Nazi authorities in Germany, they asked my family why I had left Germany. My mother and father had to tell them a lie and said that I had run away without their knowledge and against their wishes. I don't think they were entirely convinced by this cover story, but they left my parents alone afterwards and they didn't have any trouble from them again. I had volunteered to go with the medical units in Europe as I could still speak fluent German and I argued this would be useful in some of the medical situations we were going to face once there. I think one of the suits as they called them who gave approval for trained and skilled medical staff to go to Europe with the US armed forces then turns to me and says, 'what you mean you intend to help krauts over there too after all they have been doing there'? I was becoming annoyed and had to fight back my growing anger and frustration and simply remain calm and I replied to him 'we as medical staff and doctors have the moral obligation to help anyone who is suffering and in need of medical attention, we have to remain neutral even in the most terrible of circumstances'. Maybe he was testing me because he knew I was born and raised in Germany, I'm not sure but I did not react, and I remained professional. I was really happy to receive the news later that I had been accepted. I was both excited and fearful of what I would see returning to a Germany I had left what felt like an eternity ago. I had an American fiancé now and he didn't want me to go but I told him I had to do it as I knew I would be useful out there. He understood what I was saying, and, in a way, he was happy I was going but I was one of many hundreds of skilled medical staff and doctors and I was by no means special. The sea journey seemed to take forever before reaching the off-loading destination in Normandy. I had followed the news reports most days on the progress of the war up until this point. Although by the time we arrived Normandy was totally under Allied control we witnessed the aftermath of what must have been hellish fighting. In places there were still dead bodies lying on the ground rotting. We basically moved behind the advancing Allied forces and most of our work was taken up treating civilian men, women and children then more and more soldiers. The worst injuries I encountered and treated along with other doctors was after the Ardennes Battle of the winter of 1944. Some of the injuries were appalling and we had to carry out so many amputations on many young US servicemen, they begged us 'please don't cut my legs off' and things like that, they were young men who before all this madness played football, took their girlfriends to dances and led active lives.

68   The Nazi and Japanese Human Experimentation Programmes

They didn't want to be turned into cripples. I remember it was around the August of 1945 our unit was diverted as we arrived at Rathenow which lies to the west of the city of Berlin. There was talk of many sick people who were attempting to disperse into the countryside from the Sachsenhausen concentration camp which had been liberated by the Russians on 22 April. For me this was the worst part of it all not only as a doctor but as a German. The terrible state most of the prisoners of that camp were in is beyond description. Severe malnutrition, sores, diseases, broken and fractured bones, many resembled legions of the walking dead, it was like a horror story. We spent some weeks treating people and cataloguing what had caused their injuries. Some of the worst cases had been used like laboratory rats in perverse medical experiments carried out by Nazi doctors at the camp. Some of those I treated and helped to recovery before being moved on to proper hospitals had poisons injected into their bodies, one had an eye gouged out of its socket and another four had suffered having portions of flesh removed from arms and legs exposing the bones. These were serious wounds requiring specialist surgery. We made them as comfortable as possible before moving them on for surgery. Many would require skin grafts or what they called plastic surgery which were specialist disciplines. I could treat the victims of amputation, poisoning and low severity mutilation but it was a team effort involving long hours of working with a large team of doctors and nurses. We even had British nurses and medical staff working with us and made many new friends during that time. I managed to get permission to go and visit my parents for the first time in so many years, it was a painfully brief but very emotional reunion. My mother and father could not believe that their once young teenaged daughter had returned as a young woman and had helped so many poor souls to live. I returned to the USA as I could never go back to Germany after having experienced the horrors which I did. When I got married my parents came to the

USA for the ceremony and stayed with me and my husband for a couple of weeks. We would visit my parents in Germany three times a year until my father died when we made the decision to go to live in what was now West Germany again so as to help my mother. Sadly, my husband found it difficult to adapt to all of the changes and despite having a good job there we separated, he went back to the USA, and we later divorced. I continued to work as a doctor up until the age of sixty when I took retirement and began lecturing at The Charite University of Medicine in Berlin.'

Elsa Lanneberger died at the age of ninety-eight in Berlin and is survived by her two daughters, Esmée and Andrea, and her son Harvey. All three of Elsa's children followed their mother into successful medical careers.

Chapter 7

The Nuremberg Doctors' Trial

The Nuremberg Doctors' Trial was unique in bringing those within the medical profession to justice for the murder and grievous wounding of concentration camp prisoners and members of their own society. It was on 9 December 1946 that an American tribunal commenced proceedings against twenty-three leading German physicians, along with their administrative staff, for their willing participation in war crimes and crimes against humanity. The accused Nazi doctors faced four charges including:

1. Conspiracy to commit war crimes and crimes against humanity as described in counts 2 and 3.
2. War crimes: performing medical experiments, without the subject's consent, on prisoners of war and civilians of occupied countries, in the course of which experiments the defendants committed murders, brutalities, cruelties, tortures, atrocities, and other inhuman acts. Also planning and performing the mass murder of prisoners of war and civilians of occupied countries, stigmatized as aged, insane, incurably ill, deformed, and so on, by gas, lethal injections and diverse other means in nursing homes, hospitals, and asylums during the Euthanasia Program and participating in the mass murder of concentration camp inmates.
3. Crimes against humanity: committing crimes described under count 2 also on German nationals.
4. Membership in a criminal organisation, the SS.

The Nuremberg Doctors' Trial 71

In the event, the tribunal dropped count 1, stating that the charge was beyond its jurisdiction.

This was the first case of the subsequent Nuremberg proceedings. Brigadier General Telford Taylor was appointed chief of counsel during the doctors' trial. Brigadier General Taylor made the following opening statement to the proceedings:

> 'The defendants in this case are charged with murder, torture, and other atrocities committed in the name of medical science. The victims of these crimes are numbered in the hundreds of thousands. A handful only are still alive; a few survivors will appear in this courtroom. But most of these miserable victims were slaughtered outright or died in the course of the tortures to which they were subjected. For the most part they are a nameless dead. To their murderers, these wretched people were not individuals at all. They came in wholesale lot and were treated worse than animals awaiting slaughter.'

This was an emotionally charged opening statement to the court. After 140 days of proceedings, which included the personal testimonies of eighty-five witnesses and the submission of almost 1,500 documents, the American judges pronounced their verdict on 20 August 1947. Sixteen of the doctors were found guilty. Seven were sentenced to death. They were executed by hanging on 2 June 1948.

Below is a list of those who were brought before the Nuremberg Doctors' Trial, their function and their fate. Not all of them are mentioned in this book.

Paul Rostock

Rostock was Chief Surgeon of the Surgical Clinic in Berlin; Surgical Adviser to the Army; and Chief of the office for Medical Science and Research (*Amtschef der Dienststelle Medizinische Wissenschaft und*

Forschung) under the defendant Karl Brandt, Reich Commissioner for Health and Sanitation. Rostock was acquitted and died in 1956.

Wilhelm Beiglbock

Beiglbock acted as consulting physician to the German *Luftwaffe*. He was sentenced to 15 years, commuted to 10 years imprisonment. He was released on 15 December 1951 and died in 1963.

Kurt Blome

Blome acted as Deputy Reich Health Leader (*Reichsgesundheitsführer*) and Plenipotentiary for Cancer Research in the Reich Research Council. Blome was acquitted and died in 1969.

Siegfried Ruff

Ruff was Director of the Department for Aviation Medicine at the German Experimental Institute for Aviation (*Deutsche Versuchsanstalt für Luftfahrt*) and First Lieutenant in the Medical Service of the Air Force. Ruff was acquitted and continued to research and publish work in the field of aviation up until his death in 1989.

Hans-Wolfgang Romberg

Romberg was doctor on the staff of the Institute for Aviation Medicine in Berlin. Romberg was acquitted and died around 1951–2.

Konrad Schafer

Schafer was a doctor on the staff of the Institute for Aviation Medicine in Berlin. Schafer was acquitted and died in 1951.

Gerhard Rose

Rose was *Generalarzt* of the *Luftwaffe* (Major General, Medical Service of the Air Force); Vice President, Chief of the Department for Tropical Medicine, and Professor of the Robert Koch Institute, and Hygienic Adviser for Tropical Medicine to the Chief of the Medical Service of the *Luftwaffe*. Rose was sentenced to life imprisonment commuted to 20 years. He was released in 1955 and died in 1992.

Oskar Schroder

Schroder was *Generaloberstabsarzt* (Colonel General, Medical Service); Chief of Staff of the inspectorate of the Medical Service of the *Luftwaffe* (*Chef des Stabes Inspekteur des Lufwaffe-Sanitatswesens*); and Chief of the Medical Service of the *Luftwaffe* (*Chef des Sanitatswesens der Luftwaffe*). Schroder was sentenced to life imprisonment commuted to 15 years. He was released in 1954 and died in 1959.

Siegfried Handloser

Handloser was *Generaloberstabsarzt* (Lieutenant General, Medical Service); Medical Inspector of the Army (*Heeressanitatsinspekteur*); and Chief of the Medical Services of the Armed Forces (*Chef des Wehrmachtsanitatswesens*). Handloser was sentenced to life imprisonment commuted to 20 years. He was released in 1954 and died that same year.

Karl Genzken

Genzken was a *Gruppenführer* in the SS and *Genralluetnant* (Lieutenant General) in the *Waffen* SS; and Chief of the Medical Department of the *Waffen* SS (*Chef des Sanitatsamts der Waffen SS*). Genzken was sentenced to life imprisonment commuted to 20 years. He was released in April 1954 and died in 1957.

Karl Gebhardt

Gebhardt was a *Gruppenführer* in the SS and *Generalleutnant* (Lieutant General) in the *Waffen* SS; personal physician to *Reichsführer* of the SS Heinrich Himmler; Chief Surgeon of the staff of the Reich Physicians of the SS and police (*Oberster Kliniker, Reichsarzt SS und Polizei*), and President of the German Red Cross. Gebhardt was sentenced to death and was hanged on 2 June 1948.

Waldemar Hoven

Hoven was *Hauptsturmführer* (Captain) in the *Waffen* SS and Chief Doctor of the Buchenwald concentration camp. Hoven was sentenced to death and was hanged on 2 June 1948.

Georg August Weltz

Weltz was *Oberfeldarzt* in the *Luftwaffe* (Lieutenant Colonel, Medical Service, of the Air Force); and Chief of the institute for Aviation Medicine in Munich. Weltz was acquitted and died in 1963.

Victor Brack

Brack was *Oberführer* (Senior Colonel) in the SS and *Sturmbannführer* (Major) in the *Waffen* SS; and Chief Administrative Officer in the Chancellery of the Führer of the NSDAP-Nazi Party (*Oberdienstleiter, Kanzlei des Führers der NSDAP*). Brack was sentenced to death and was hanged on 2 June 1948.

Helmut Poppendick

Poppendick was *Oberführer* (Senior Colonel) in the SS; and Chief of the Personal Staff of the Reich Physcians SS and Police (*Chef des Personlichen Stabes des Reichsarztes SS und Polizei*). Poppendick was sentenced to 10 years imprisonment and was released in 1951 and died in 1994.

Joachim Mrugowsky

Mrugowsky was *Oberführer* (Senior Colonel) in the *Waffen* SS; Chief Hygienist of the Reich Physician SS and Police (*Oberster Hygieniker, Reichsarzt SS und Polizei*); and Chief of the Hygienic Institute of the *Waffen* SS (*Chef des Hygienischen Institutes der Waffen SS*). Mrugowsky was sentenced to death and was hanged on 2 June 1948.

Karl Brandt

Brandt was personal physician to Adolf Hitler, *Gruppenführer* in the SS and *Generaleutnant* (Lieutenant General) in the *Waffen* SS; Reich Commissioner for Health and Sanitation (*Reichskommissar für Sanitäts und Gesundheitswesen*); and member of the Reich Research Council (*Reichsforschungsrat*). Brandt was sentenced to death and was hanged on 2 June 1948.

Herta Oberheuser

Oberheuser was a physician at the Ravensbruck concentration camp; and Assistant Physician to the defendant Gebhardt at the hospital at Hohenlychen. Oberheuser was sentenced to 20 years imprisonment, commuted to 10 years. She was released in 1952 and died in 1978.

Adolf Pokorny

Pokorny was a physician specialising in skin and venereal diseases. He was acquitted.

76 The Nazi and Japanese Human Experimentation Programmes

Hermann Becker-Freyseng

Freyseng was *Stabsarzt* in the *Luftwaffe* (Captain, Medical Service of the Air Force); and Chief of the Department for Aviation Medicine of the Chief of the Medical Service of the *Luftwaffe*. Freyseng was sentenced to 20 years imprisonment commuted to 10 years. Freyseng was released in 1952 and died in 1961.

Wolfram Sievers

Sievers was *Standartenführer* (Colonel) in the SS. Reich Manager of the Ahnenerbe Society and Director of its Institute for Military Scientific Research (*Institut für Wehrwissenschaftliche Zweckforschung*), and Deputy Chairman of the Managing Board of Directors of the Reich Research Council. Sievers was sentenced to death and was hanged on 2 June 1948.

Rudolf Brandt

Brandt was *Standartenführer* (Colonel) in the *Allgemeine* SS, Personal Administrative Officer to the *Reichsführer* of the SS Heinrich Himmler (*Personlicher Referent von Himmler*), and Ministerial Counsellor and Chief of the Ministerial Office in the Reich Ministry of the Interior. Brandt was sentenced to death and was hanged on 2 June 1948.

Fritz Fischer

Fischer was *Sturmbannführer* (Major) in the *Waffen* SS; and Assistant Physician to the defendant Gebhardt at the hospital at Hohenlychen. Fischer was sentenced to life imprisonment commuted to 15 years. He was released in March 1954 and died in 2003.

All of the criminals sentenced to death were hanged at Landsberg Prison on 2 June 1948, but what became of Carl Clauberg, Eduard Wirths, Horst Schumann, Ernst Holzlohner, Sigmund Rascher, Horst Fischer, Hermann Stieve and Otmar Freiherr von Verschuer?

Carl Clauberg

With the Red Army advancing towards Auschwitz, Carl Clauberg fled the camp, moving on to the Ravensbruck concentration camp where he continued his experiments on Romani women. When Russian troops arrived at the Ravensbruck camp in 1945 Clauberg was arrested there. After the end of the Second World War Clauberg was put on trial in the Soviet Union and was sentenced to 25 years in prison. In 1955 he was released (but not pardoned) by the Soviet Union under the Adenauer-Bulganin prisoner exchange agreement, with the final group of around 10,000 prisoners of war and civilian internees. Clauberg returned to West Germany where for some reason he was reinstated at his former clinic, based on his pre-war scientific output. Bizarre behaviour, including openly boasting of his 'achievements' in 'developing a new sterilization technique at the Auschwitz concentration camp', destroyed any chance he might have had of staying unnoticed. After a public outcry among concentration camp survivors in 1955 Clauberg was arrested by the West German authorities but died before his trial, which was scheduled for 9 August 1957 in Kiel.

Eduard Wirths

Eduard Wirths was captured by the Allies at the end of the Second World War and held in custody by the British forces. Late on 20 September 1945 Wirths, fearful of facing trial for his part in Nazi war crimes, committed suicide, ironically by hanging. Had he not, it is likely the hangman would have saved him the trouble of doing it himself.

Horst Schumann

Horst Schumann fled Germany at the end of the war in 1945. He was later discovered in hiding in Ghana and was subsequently extradited from Ghana to West Germany. The trial against him opened on 23 September 1970. Schumann was charged with killing some 30,000

78   The Nazi and Japanese Human Experimentation Programmes

Jews, but Schumann admitted to killing as many as 80,000 Jews, saying that he 'had no numbers'. However, Schumann was released from prison on 29 July 1972 due to a heart condition and deteriorating health. He died on 5 May 1983, eleven years after his release from prison.

Ernst Holzlohner

Ernst Holzlohner was captured by British forces at the end of the war and was another who committed suicide, taking his own life in June 1945 to avoid almost certain execution.

Sigmund Rascher

Sigmund Rascher was detained at the Buchenwald concentration camp following his arrest in 1944, after falling foul of SS Chief Heinrich Himmler. Rascher had been accused of financial irregularities, the murder of his former lab assistant, and scientific fraud. Rascher was detained at Buchenwald until the evacuation of the camp in April 1945. He and other prisoners were then taken to Dachau. Rascher was executed by shooting on 26 April 1945 by German soldiers, three days before the camp was liberated by American troops.

Horst Fischer

At the war's end in 1945 Horst Fischer was able to get his SS blood group tattoo removed to help him avoid detection by the Allied authorities. He continued his medical career in the German Democratic Republic (DDR) for a period of twenty years. During this time Fischer married, had four children and lived the life of any ordinary middle-class citizen. In 1959 West German officials received material on Fischer's activities at Auschwitz. A warrant was issued for his arrest on 6 April 1960, but his whereabouts could not be ascertained. In the bureaucratic muddle which followed the East German government reprimanded

The Nuremberg Doctors' Trial   79

the Stasi (Ministry for State Security) for failing to track down any Auschwitz personnel since the 1950s. Fischer was eventually caught and his trial began on 10 March 1966. The trial lasted for one week and Fischer was found guilty of crimes against humanity. Fischer had assumed that if he cooperated fully with the authorities that he might be spared execution and be handed a life sentence in prison instead. This was somewhat naïve, and on 8 July 1966 Fischer was executed by guillotine at Leipzig. His remains were cremated and buried in an unmarked grave.

Hermann Stieve

Hermann Stieve was never held to account for his participation in the Nazi medical experimentation programme. He had received corpses and human organs, fully aware that they had originated from murdered prisoners in the Nazi concentration camps. He knew what had happened to the prisoners but continued his work with their blood on his hands. However, this did not hamper his later career. In the years after the Second World War he was awarded many accolades and one institution even had a bust of him erected in his honour. Stieve died on 5 September 1952 at the age of sixty-six in West Berlin.

Emil Gelny

Little information exists about the movements of Nazi doctor Emil Gelny after the Second World War. It was Gelny who had remarked that the inmates of the Gugging Asylum were nothing more than 'useless mouths', a phrase the Nazis often used thereafter when referring to the mentally ill or severely physically disabled. Gelny appeared to vanish into thin air after the war, possibly with the assistance of influential friends. It is known that he turned up in Syria and later Iraq, where he was welcomed and able to practice medicine again. He died in Baghdad, Iraq in 1961.

Otmar Freiherr von Verschuer

After the war von Verschuer claimed to have turned his back on Nazi beliefs, but many remained unconvinced. Despite his Nazi history, von Verschuer was awarded at least six honours in the post-war years. He never appeared in court to answer for his activities in the Third Reich during the Second World War and he was killed in a car accident in 1969.

Even today, many decades after the end of the Second World War, the legacy of the Nazi human experiment programme continues to rear its ugly head. In 2015 a researcher in France uncovered test tubes at Strasbourg medical school which were found to contain human samples from the Holocaust, apparently collected by the Nazi physician August Hirt. The test tubes and jars contained human tissue from eighty-six Jews who had been gassed primarily so that their bodies could be used for biological and anatomical research. The samples had been retained in the hope that they could form part of the evidence in a prosecution case against Hirt, but when French staff at the facility were replaced the samples were locked away and appear to have been forgotten. Hirt committed suicide so could never be brought to trial for his crimes. The tissue samples have since been handed over to the Strasbourg Jewish community for eventual burial in the city.

Also in 2015, human brain samples were discovered at the Max Planck Psychiatric Institute in Munich during construction work. During the Holocaust the institute regularly received samples of human organs, bones and tissue from murdered Holocaust victims. It was confirmed that these samples were among those collected by Dr Josef Mengele and his colleagues specifically for analysis at the lab formerly known as the Kaiser Wilhelm Institute. The findings proved something of an embarrassment for the institute, and were not made public for some time, which has also drawn criticism.

In 2016 in Berlin 300 tissue samples were discovered among the belongings of Nazi physician Hermann Stieve, who has already been discussed. The tissue samples had been removed from the corpses of men and women who had opposed the Nazis or Stieve himself. Most had been executed by guillotine and most of the victims were female. This reiterated the level of close cooperation that had existed between the Nazi justice system and the Berlin anatomy department. Some of the tissue samples had been so meticulously labelled by the Nazi physicians that the identities of the victims were easily ascertained. Their names were not made public as their families asked that they remain anonymous.

In 2014, during road works in Berlin's Dahlem district, a large number of human bones were unearthed in close proximity to a site where Nazi physicians had carried out research into human body parts during the Second World War. The road works were within the property of the Berlin State University. Among the remains uncovered by workmen were numerous fractured skulls, teeth, vertebrae and other bones including those identified as having come from children. In a sense Germany is one mass graveyard, and the remains of those murdered by the Nazis are constantly being discovered when work begins on the construction of new buildings and/or roadways. It is likely, due to the sheer scale of the Nazi human medical experimentation programme of the Second World War, that many more victims will be discovered over time. It is yet another dreadful legacy of a corrupt regime.

The testimonies below were collected from living individuals who were subjected to Nazi medical experiments and who were identified by the Conference on Jewish Material Claims Against Germany. These testimonies, and those of other identified individuals, remain on record with the United States Holocaust Memorial Museum, Washington DC, Yad Vashem (in Israel) and in other Holocaust institutions. The victims wanted their experiences to be known and become a part of the historical record, but asked that their names remain private due to the sensitivity of the material.

82　The Nazi and Japanese Human Experimentation Programmes

Miss A, now aged 83, was a prisoner at Auschwitz between April and May 1943. She recalled:

'The experiment was done to me in Auschwitz, Block 10. The experiment was done on my uterus. I was given shots in my uterus and as a result of that I was fainting from severe pain for a year and a half. Years later Professor Hirsch from the hospital in Tzrifin examined me and said that my uterus became as a uterus of a four-year-old child and that my ovaries had shrank.'

Mr G, now aged 82, was at Rabka bei Zakopane in 1942 and recalled:

'In 1940–41 we were living in Krakow, Poland. The Nazis started to build the ghetto. My father finds a house in the province, in between Krakow and Zakopane. The village is called Rabka. This happened because we did not want to go to the ghetto. The SS and Gestapo robbed all of our possessions from the villa we lived in. What I am about to write has never been heard before. Me and a Jewish American who held a US passport were subjected to medical experiments. German Shepherd dogs which belonged to the SS commander Obersturmführer Rosenbaum were set upon us. Afterwards our wounds were examined as the dogs had bitten us. It was reported the dogs had some form of poison placed in their teeth. Flesh was taken from my legs so as the doctors could examine it. After some time, I was able to escape fleeing first to a peasant village – afterwards to a friend living in Krakow. There my wounded legs started to heal. As a result of the dog bites and the poison the wounds developed into cancer. During August 1962 and November 1962, I was operated on in the cancer institute and was treated at Gliwice in Poland.'

Mr B, now aged 76 was at Melk between September 1944 and January 1945 and recalled:

The Nuremberg Doctors' Trial   83

'In Revier, Melk, there was a concentration and labour camp there. There was an SS doctor and nurses all of whom wore SS uniforms and from time-to-time civilians came to visit and it may be that these civilians were something to do with drug manufacturers. Without any reason they made a cut, about ten centimetres long and two centimetres wide in my arm above the palm of my hand. Today I understand that the surgery that was done on me without any anaesthesia was done purposely with tools that had not been sterilized beforehand. This was done deliberately to cause infection. At the time they kept changing the bandages with different medicated creams and liquids. The bandage was not wrapped around my arm but just placed over the wound. Every day they examined the cut and each time the cut was about to heal, they would reopen it and start the whole process again. Once in a while civilians would come to check us and the charts; they made some remarks and gave orders. A part of the experiment was also observation, and they also checked our ability to work with the wound. After we were transferred to Ebensee I got lucky and a paramedic who worked in the clinic took care of me and treated my wound. The final treatment was done in an American military hospital at Linz in Austria. After my release the doctors said that I was very lucky. There are scars still today and much pain and restricted mobility in my arm.'

Ms B, now aged 78, was at Auschwitz from April 1944 to September 1944 and recalled:

'I was put into barrack number 10 at Auschwitz in April 1944. After a month or so of being in barrack number 10, I as well as the other female prisoners were no longer able to menstruate each month. And we all experienced a terrible rash. First pus-filled blisters appeared and these then turned into sores. In some cases, the rash occurred on both of my arms and my chest. In the morning and the night, we were lined up for approximately two hours for roll call. During this time Dr Mengele came once or twice a week and he pulled out the sick and the weak from the line and those that were pulled out were never seen again. It was necessary to make sure that the entire body was covered so Mengele would not see even one sore, if he had our lives would be over. Dr Gisela Perl assisted Mengele throughout the day. However, at night Dr Perl came into the barracks and administered an ointment with glue like consistency to every sore in order to heal this horrific rash. Dr Perl came to barracks number 10 periodically and also went to other barracks to administer this ointment. The rash needed several weeks to clear up; however, it would often return a few days later. In Auschwitz, there was a belief among the female prisoners that the soup that we were given to eat was drugged and the drug was the reason why we suffered from this terrible rash. Without Dr Perl's medical knowledge and willingness to risk her life by helping us, it would have been impossible to know what would have happened to us female prisoners. I lived in Sighet, the same town as Dr Perl, until I was sixteen, when I was sent away to the ghetto. I remember what a wonderful reputation she had, and how well known she was in our area. My mother was her patient, and my grandmother went to her husband, Dr Krauss, who was an internist.

It is interesting to note that Dr Gisella Perl was a Hungarian Jewish gynaecologist who was deported to Auschwitz in 1944. She helped hundreds of women during her time at the camp with the barest of necessities for practising medicine. She is one of the many unsung heroes of the Nazi Holocaust. Dr Gisella Perl died on 16 December 1988 at her home in Herzliya, Israel.

Mrs M, now aged 73, was at Auschwitz from June 1944 to May 1945. She recalled:

The Nuremberg Doctors' Trial   85

'I suffered immense pain and cruelty from the experiments. They were inhuman, but because of them I survived. As bad as the experiments were without them, I would not be here today to write this. Now that I am emotionally stronger, I would like to describe a little more detail about the horrible experiments that no matter how hard I try I shall never get over for as long as I live. I was born November 23rd, 1930. I had been at Auschwitz five weeks and was separated from my family, my parents, two brothers and two sisters when Dr Mengele pulled me out of a queue as we were on the way from the C-lager camp to the gas chambers. I was the only one picked that day personally by Mengele and his assistant. They took me to his laboratory, where I met other children. They were screaming from pain. Their bodies were black and blue and covered in blood. I collapsed from the horror, and I fainted. A bucket of cold water was thrown over me to revive me. As soon as I stood up, I was whipped with a leather whip which broke my flesh, then I was told the whipping was a sample of what I would receive if I did not follow instructions and orders. I was used as a guinea pig for medical experiments. I was never given painkillers or anaesthetic. Every single day I suffered excruciating pain. I was injected with drugs and chemicals. My body most of the time was connected to tubes which inserted drugs into my body. Many days I was tied up for hours. Some days they made cuts into my body leaving the wounds open for them to study. Most of the time I was given nothing to eat. Every day we woke up and the place was empty. We were left with open infected wounds and no food. We were all half dead with no energy or life left in us. When the Russians arrived, they tried to shake me to see if I was alive or dead. They felt a tiny beat in my heart and quickly picked me up and took me to hospital.'

Mr K, now aged 80, was at Auschwitz from 1942 to 1945 and recalled:

86   The Nazi and Japanese Human Experimentation Programmes

'As soon as I arrived at Auschwitz I was taken into a room and there I was undressed and made to kneel down on my hands and knees. The SS officer who was probably a doctor as he was dressed in a white surgical robe, shoved an iron stick which had a handle on its end right into my rectum. He then turned the stick which caused an involuntary ejaculation of sperm. A female SS officer who was assisting this man held two pieces of glass underneath my genitals in order to collect a sample of my sperm for the lab. They then made me stand on a special machine that gave electric shocks to both sides of my genitals until again sperm was ejaculated. After the liberation I was taken to the Sanatorium Gauting near Munich. There I was bedridden for almost a year starting with a weight of only thirty kilograms. During that year I was operated on for a serious medical condition.'

Mr K's account is one of several I have encountered referring to the stimulation of the sexual organs using electrical currents. This appears to have occurred in many of the concentration camps. Female prisoners were often restrained before having electrical plugs inserted into their anus or vagina before electrical currents of varying strengths were then passed through the plugs. For males this appears to have been some crude method of making them ejaculate, and the sperm was then collected and taken for analysis. Why the procedure was carried out on females is not entirely clear, and there remains the gruesome possibility that it was simply for the gratification of the doctors involved. A German witness I interviewed for a previous work (*Sex Under the Swastika*) had seen two such experiments. She noted that in both cases the restrained women fought desperately to control themselves, trying to prevent any reaction being apparent to the SS doctors who were watching and controlling the current being applied to their bodies.

The witness told me that as the current was increased via a dial on a grey metal control panel, a needle on a kind of clock face would move each time the current was increased. As the current was increased the women, she noted, would arch their backs violently and moan as if they were being stimulated to orgasm. What may have initially been bearable sensations soon became painful as the current was turned up. When the doctors observing the procedure felt that the prisoner had received enough current, it would be switched off. The prisoner would then be examined by the doctors internally before being released and sent back to the barracks. In the two cases mentioned by my witness both women were brought back the next day to undergo the same procedure and as a result both women died. In one case a female prisoner was brought in strapped down again with her wrists above her head and with her back flat against the table and legs strapped down and held apart. An electrode was inserted into her vagina and a wire was placed on her clitoris by means of a small metal clamp. An electrical current was then administered, the woman bravely gave no reaction as the voltage was increased. She bit down so hard on her bottom lip that it began to bleed quite profusely, her body began to convulse but she fought hard to give no reaction to those doctors watching. The dial on the control panel was then turned up to what must have been its maximum level and held the there. The witness to this particular experiment told me that by the time the doctors had finished there was a slight smell of burning flesh in the air.

On another occasion a male prisoner was brought in, he was ordered to kneel down on all fours before being fastened into the position by means of a head restraint and heavy leather straps. An electrode was pushed into his anus until only the electrical wire could be seen, two more electrodes were placed one on each of his testicles. A current was then passed through the electrical wires and the witness saw how the prisoner's penis became erect. At this phase of the experiment (if one could call it that) one of the female SS doctors placed a black rubber glove on her right hand. It was one of those heavy-duty rubber gloves which went almost up the entire arm. The current was switched off for approximately 50 seconds as the female SS doctor with her gloved right hand then proceeded to masturbate the prone prisoner. She did this

88   The Nazi and Japanese Human Experimentation Programmes

very firmly and quickly and moments before the prisoner ejaculated, she removed her hand, and the current was switched back on. Within a few seconds the prisoner without any further physical stimulation ejaculated heavily and the female SS doctor had placed a glass tubular vase beneath the prisoner's penis in order to catch the fluid. The doctors laughed and remarked that it was "just like milking a cow". It was an extremely degrading and humiliating experiment for the male prisoner, but it was one of many such experiments which can only best be described as rape experiments. There were some of the male prisoners who were brought in to undergo this procedure who began to protest violently once they had an idea of what was going to be done to them. Another witness I spoke to again for a previous work focussing on the subject told me that the doctors involved had a simple way of subduing a troublesome male prisoner prior to this procedure. It was not only via the heavy leather straps and buckles used to restrain them but the threat of being castrated if they gave the doctors any trouble. On at least one instance the witness did see a male prisoner castrated after the procedure had been carried out and sufficient voltage had been administered to render the prisoner incapable of even moving, much like a hog prior to having its throat cut in a slaughterhouse. The witness described how an ordinary butchers type knife was used to castrate the prisoner who was then left on the floor in agony to die. The corpse was taken away for incineration and two female prisoners were brought in with mops and buckets to clean up the blood from the floor. As the women cleaned up the blood other prisoners were brought in, and the procedure carried out while they were present in the room. The SS doctors present argued that these two Jewish women will be dead soon anyway and will not survive to tell the tale.

These experiments were conducted at Auschwitz and other concentration camps where inmates were selected for medical experimentation. It was not only older men and women who were selected for these rape experiments, but young girls and boys too. It was also revealed to me by the witness I interviewed that the young

Franz Joseph Gall. The father of phrenology.

Elsa Lanneberger. (*Author's Collection*)

Nazi doctor Carl Clauberg. (*Holocaust Archive*)

Reichsführer of the SS Heinrich Himmler. (*Wikimedia*)

Eduard Wirths. (*Wikimedia*)

Horst Fischer. (*Wikimedia*)

Horst Schumann. (*Wikimedia*)

Doctor Herta Oberheuser. (*Holocaust Archive*)

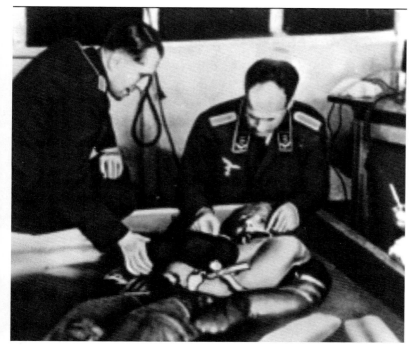

Holzlohner and Rascher experimenting with freezing water using a concentration camp prisoner. (*Holocaust Archive*)

Josef Mengele at the Auschwitz camp in SS uniform. (*Holocaust Archive*)

Josef Mengele's identification document photo, taken in Argentina, 1956. (*Holocaust Archive*)

Exhibition titled 'Physical and Emotional Appearance of The Jews' at the Museum of Natural History, Vienna, 1939. (*Holocaust Archive*)

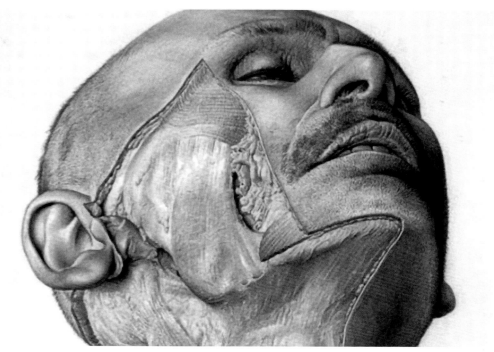

Illustration from Pernkopf's *Topographic Anatomy of Man*.

Member of the SS *Totenkopfverbande*.

Nazi dissection table.
(*Holocaust Archive*)

Girls learning genetics and racial characteristics at the Berlin School for the Blind. These same girls were later sterilized.

Doctor Gisella Perl. One of the unsung heroes of Auschwitz. (*Wikimedia*)

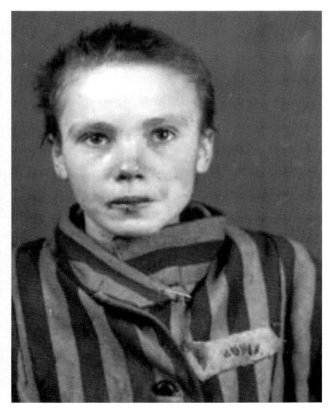

Fourteen-year-old Czeslawa Kwoka. (*Holocaust Archive*)

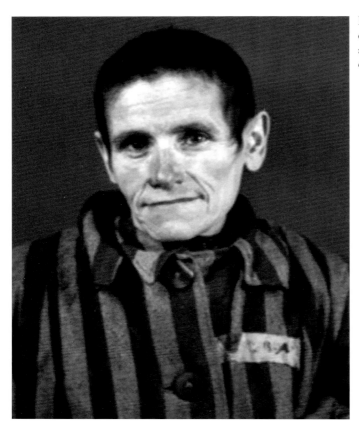

Katarzyna Kwoka, mother of Czeslawa, murdered at Auschwitz prior to her daughter. (*Holocaust Archive*)

Crystaline carbolic acid used to murder prisoners at Auschwitz.

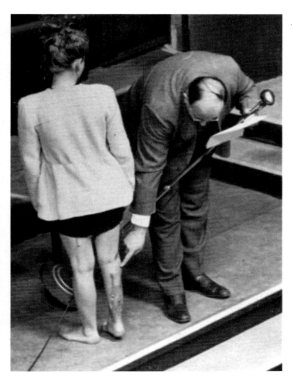

Jadwiga Dzido shows scars on her leg from medical experiments at the Nazi Doctors' Trial.

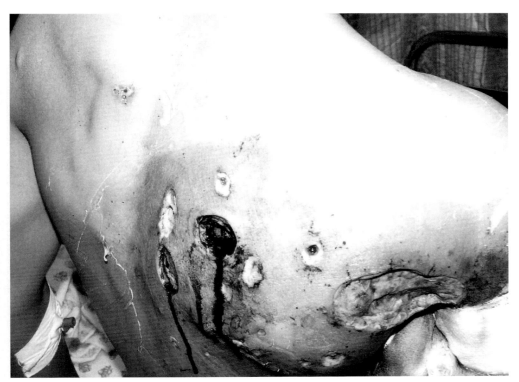

White phosphorous burns on a prisoner's back.

Japanese General Shiro Ishii pictured here in military uniform. (*Wikimedia*)

Japanese General Shiro Ishii pictured here attending a post-Second World War Unit 731 veterans' association reunion.